BOAR

Tom Branfoot is a poet and critic from Bradford. He is the writer-in-residence at Manchester Cathedral and a recipient of the New Poets Prize 2022. He organises the poetry reading series More Song at The Record Café in Bradford. *This Is Not an Epiphany,* Tom's second pamphlet of poetry, is published by Smith|Doorstop.

Praise for *boar*

Sharp as a cutting implement, thoughtful as a woodland pause, Branfoot's assured yet disturbing poems bring history home: its quiet atrocities, its local and poetic languages, its possible organization into forms of hope. I love the flow: from medieval beast lore to critical modern observation; the underground beck, the struggling coffee shop. This writing haunts and needles us, like Alan Garner or Barry MacSweeney.
— Anthony (Vahni) Capildeo, *Like a Tree, Walking*

Tom Branfoot's latest pamphlet roots out the brutal buried histories of the Bradford Boar as a dark mirror of a broken present. In an arresting idiom ventriloquising Middle English, Branfoot stalks the boar's fateful path through the ages of social oppression and ecological degradation. In this vision, the boar's unruly energy, once condemned as sinful desire, becomes a revolutionary blazon for our 'common condition' where the tongueless boar evokes the alienated voice of the poet. If haunted by how history happens 'so close to home', this bold book knows that it is nevertheless 'impossible to eradicate / wildenes' and exhorts us ultimately to become 'more human more boar'.
— Scott Thurston, *Phrases Towards a Kinepoetics*

Out of the wandring wood of Bradford's past emerges Tom Branfoot's roborant boar: mutilated, deviant, irrepressible, 'slippery / as heritage' and often disturbingly, suddenly, human. Tongueless yet articulate, it beats a path through cherished legend, 'unstable / masculinities' and generations of state violence. In poems which marshal luminous archival detail, flashes of contemporary despair and the boar's own 'ambiguous' traces into 'a new constellation', Branfoot urges us to rage for the devastated commons, to face 'our common condition now' and to remember that 'it is impossible to eradicate / wildenes'.
— Joseph Minden, *Backlogues*

In *boar*, Tom Branfoot furnishes Bradford with the return of the medieval, a scene (or is it sin?) of dispossession that body and mind still confront at every locked gate, every barbed wired interstice and mulched boundary of the city. This is a space that is both painfully specific — in its suicides, riots and neglect — yet riven with the animal desire of the boar-brute-peasant-commoner. It falls to the voice of this wild history to 'constitute a new constellation', to glean forth a poetic heraldry of the dispossessed that is louder, more brutal and more generous than the powers that have tried to repress it. This is Bradford entering the cosmos of its genuine making.
— Mau Baiocco, *The Resting Acrobats*

Tom Branfoot's *boar* is a work of gorgeous, clear-eyed contradictions. At times it feels like an erasure but with no obvious source text — a palimpsest we can't be sure is a palimpsest. boar is paradoxical. It conjures all the atmosphere of a literary retelling, but nevertheless persists and revels in its newness. It's agile, strange, and clever and funny. Glory be to this 'thirsty… bristly…purple milk thistle brute.
— Susannah Dickey, *Common Decency*

boar

Tom Branfoot

Broken Sleep Books

The brute is always saying something,
is saying give me the labor of your body,
not the work of your hands.
   — Anne Boyer, *Garments Against Women*

& the town is yours
o gasping swine
   — Sean Bonney, *The Commons*

ISBN: 978-1-915760-27-2

Cover designed by Aaron Kent

Edited and typeset by Aaron Kent

Broken Sleep Books Ltd
Rhydwen
Talgarreg
Ceredigion
SA44 4HB

Broken Sleep Books Ltd
Fair View
St Georges Road
Cornwall
PL26 7YH

Contents

crest

the main components of the story are depicted
on the City of Bradford crest

a boar's head sans tongue   an oak tree to represent a wood
a well to embody a spring   & three horns for the heirs

     of Northrop
          who went each year to the Market Place

with a hunting dog
on St Martin's Day

          to blow three times
          & rejoice of the king

          (at what point does ritual
          become tradition)

scene

legend dates to the 14th century
when Bradford was

                                        owned

                    by the Plantagenets

          by John of Gaunt   Duke of Lancaster

after the Norman Conquest
Bradford was part of the Ilbert de Lacy holdings

               (who travelled to Britain
                      with William the Conqueror)

John of Gaunt inherited the de Lacy holdings   by way
of an auspicious marriage
to Henry 1st Duke of Lancaster's eldest daughter
          Blanche of Lancaster

bradford

Bradford Dale contained several manors
which are now part of the City

      Bolton   Eccleshill   Bowling   Magna Horton   Horton
      Clayton   Thornton   Allerton   Heaton   Manningham

         surrounded the small town

inhabitants of these manors
would travel to the town
for church services
    & to trade in its markets

               the church
        was the only one in the area
      & markets were held
         in its yard

streams flowed
down to meet Bradford Beck
which provided a power source
           water & fish for the town

the hillsides were treelined
    a wildness
depleted

         Cliffe Wood

   stretched   to the north of the church
          along the banks of the Beck to the Aire

boar

during the Middle Ages   many areas
of the country
were infested with wild boars

            they were a danger to the inhabitants
                & many people were killed by them

a male boar can weigh up to 200 kilograms

one such boar
inhabited Cliffe Wood

                            & causing grief
                                    for any person

            travelling by foot
            from Manningham   to Bradford

        legend says that the Lord of the Manor offered a reward

of three messuages
    & six bovates of land

                        to anyone who could kill the boar

        the land exists today
            as Hunt Yard
                the story does not state

                            which Lord this was

    it may have been John of Gaunt

on one of his visits to the town

the route

from his castle

in Pontefract

to his castle

in Lancaster

took him
straight through
Bradford Dale

northrop

an inhabitant of Manningham   reportedly a member
of the Northrop family   was walking
through Cliffe Wood near the church
when he saw the boar   drinking   from a well

Northrop was armed
& speared the boar   killing it instantly

                                                 a dilemma

having been on an errand   he could not
go directly to claim the reward

           Northrop cut out the boar's tongue
  to evidence his hunt

                         placed it in his pouch
                                retrieved his spear
                        & went on his way

shortly afterwards
  another man came along the road
& saw the dead boar

                    he did not notice
         the missing tongue
            & decided to claim the reward

the boar was far too burdensome
to carry   so he beheaded the brute

& made his way to the manor
where the reward was to be presented

the chancer was received heroically

                                         until Northrop appeared

              producing the rough tongue
proving he had slain
    the wild boar

  & claimed his rightful reward

brute ode

o tongueless brute

thirsty brute   bristly brute

purple milk thistle brute

thicke-necked brute

emancipated brute

brute of the well

o terrorist brute

anarchist brute

brute of the woods

arboreal brute

o gnashynge brute

other-than-human brute   open field brute

o landed brute

brute of the blazon

itinerant brute

leveller brute

ravenous brute

killable brute

carrion-devourynge brute

irredeemable brute

ambiguous brute

brute
ravaged brute   of lore

golden bristles brute

boardoze the hedgerows

o lazarus brute   o wund-maker brute

church in the woods

I stand outside the cathedral   which was wooded
once   helicopters gull over

the gardener's bonnet   soundynge emergency
mid-century gothic signage   as if god

was a typographer   helle-fearynge peasants
worked here for free   before evensong

poverty stays in the soil like sanctity   *the parish church*
was known   as the church in the woods

unseasonable warmth   acer leaves brownynge
the Clean Air Zone   weathercock still

as a severed tongue   carpark clouded with National
Trust stickers   I used to enter every church I passed

the word itself steepled with aitches
now I'm apathetic   uninterested in powers

that revoke love in the blink   of a sun
tithe barns full of tongues   dry as controlled demolition

I sit on a dark wooden bench in the autumnal yard
opposite   the de Lacy community centre

the paradox of tonguelessness is voice
what is our common   condition now

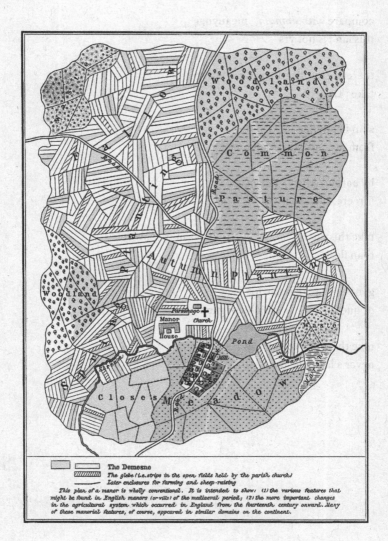

The Demesne

The glebe (i.e. strips in the open fields held by the parish church)

Later enclosures for farming and sheep-raising

This plan of a manor is wholly conventional. It is intended to show: (1) the various features that might be found in English manors (or vills) of the mediaeval period, (2) the more important changes in the agricultural system which occurred in England from the fourteenth century onward. Many of these manorial features, of course, appeared in similar domains on the continent.

demesne

compare with *domain*   meanynge
this land is not yrs

there are implications to exclusion
take this field

skin flappynge
from my gaol shredded

by barbed wire   durynge
  recreational activity

take this duchy   thynges more covert
than flesh

generatynge revenue for kyng
or quene   or john of gaunt

take the ryght to destroy
never a lastynge bone

hoof

pilgrimynge to sites   you roamed
          wi flaysome hooves
   where bonnie wimmin wackered
at the sight   o your tusks

waist deep
            in hip-breear
woodgatherynge in the commons
turned brownfield sites
wells replaced wi taps   reservoirs
at lower levels
    than predicted
this dreedist somer   no reyn
you couldn't beliven here
now   the wold is fellen

no county for bristle and snaht
   they thought you   brute
    doing what they did to ahr land
wi walls wi lords and wi law

it made sense for the hunter to find out all he could about his quarry

bothrin over brass   northrop
waited by the well

wantynge to ken   all he could abaht
his quarry   needynge reward

somethynge to warm his breste
at nyght his bairns

croodled up in their cruck
house   beastless

someone told him
afore the nature o these feral pigs

ther crueltye and risk
when ther tusks are blunting   they seeketh

a herb called *origanum* and gnaweth it
and cheweth it and cleanse

the roots of his teeth by virtue thereof
like slaghte for a fang of land

I am cutten from the same silk

cloth as strykynge workers
     from Manningham Mill
theyr paye cleaved

on Cristemasse Eve 1890
this poem   leves a stone for them
    on the banks of Bradford Beck

drownen   in its brackish water
with england deed
europe deed   the royal remnants   deed

austerity is the absence of a thynge
    once known
a cavity severe with ice

what I'd give to be lovelye and cleane
not drynken at Jacob's Well
unable   to quellen the minde

hangynge up my cote of armes
unshawen
wracked with tumulte

midwynter nyght   a caterwaul of crowes
leven a wund
when yu closen the dore

in these handen   a smal animal died
of fryht   palme lynes
crystallysed with blod

leven a stone on this tender cairn
　　　　love being
monolythik

remember to leven
　　　　leavynge being luve
for the greater goode　　being monotheystik

cygnet

rings of clouded funnel
moon the copse
of ivied sycamore
around the hospital's
mulch boundary
each year they take
it back
to brickwork
each suicide
reduces the treeline
no walker
wishes to find
a noose
drooping
with the pearlike
weight of man
back before
this lasting fog
we peered through
the trees
glimpsed caged
bodies grieving
a battery farm
of patrilineal
shame and
crown shyness
occasionally
inmates would escape
throwing tiles
from the roof
or bolting

through pastures
it was an event
we should be scared
threatened by
unstable
masculinities
in the legends
all ferocious wild
boars are male
identified
with sin
unfettered desire
black and ugly
like those who
lost the light
they delight
in filth and flesh
inflamed
with venereal rage

more than more

it was believed   in the myddle ages   that
wild boar's bristles were as hard as precious
metal   that an apple could be dropped on
to each of their speared hairs remainynge like
a creaturely chrystyngle   in wynter nyght
if domesticatede pigs are released
into the wild   they recover ferality
tusks and razored bristles recrudesce
it is impossible to eradicate
wildenes   helyxed into wyn darke blod
do you not feel this trewe to humans
too this prymeval desire   nearynge the banks
of the beck   to drinketh of the water
and become more human more boar

labor omnia vincit

why did the lord of the manor offer a plot of land to whoever killed the
boar   if the boar was terrorising crops and increasing risk to harvest
farmers would have been dissatisfied   tremors of the peasant's revolt
already in the air   poll tax   and tithe   barns   the reward of
unpeasanting   three messuages and six bovates   whether this
was john of gaunt or his representative matters little   *work conquers
all* reads the crest   have we heard that before   without getting all
marxist   our historical conjuncture   parallels this time   rising rents
inflationary prices   unpayable bills   death of the reigning monarch
tax cuts for the 1%   the failure of growth   this is unprecedented
form for unprecedented times give me a well to drink from and I'll
share it with you without spears through the side   tongue mutilation
if the boar was tremors   land matters little   all my ifs are spitless
wasted on progress industry humanity

Labore omnia vincit.
BRADFORD.

constellate

windows condensated   with crowded
bodies   between what sky is cleare
i constitute   a new constellation
projected in wynter   nyght
tusks glent   strung with silk
each eye fisted   through cloudcover
revealynge the hereafter   bristlynge
with astigmatic coruscation
you can feel the yvel   toniht beneath
moonlyght's moist & corrugated stryfe
beneath the blysful snaht   i gaze out
dark arvum   flankynge the road
its porcine glyph   i etch
into the rattlynge   chiaroscuro
agitated by globules   of past & present
passengers   meet me by the oak
of your hooves   ryghten this rule
i fear for carnage   cloven countries

lost commons

i would love to stryke john of gaunt
seeing as i can't ransack
the savoy palace

and tear to pieces cloth of gold
rich and silver tapestries

break up the furniture   crush his plates
grind his jewels and precious
stones under foot

seeing as we can't revolt
                (under the police crimes and
        sentencing courts act)

i would place a sharpened tusk
to his plantagenet pharynx

and demand the commoning
of crown land
i would glue myself to his lineage

everyone i love lives in this ancient riding
we could start an agricultural commune

in that house
in the middle of the M62
and refuse to move

I work in a former abattoir

code switching
like it's going
out of fashion
yawns
sieved through
my terrazzo mouth
sunless mornings
one bus
every hour
peopled with rage
rainwaxed floors
slippery
as heritage
once I would have
cut myself
like a service
it is right to show
buoyancy
in the workplace
targeted measures
for evisceration
no one can take
my obscure folk
records away
the slaughterhouse
is a luxury
shopping experience
naturally
I hitch night
to the last bus's
tow bar

pressed like a flower
against carcasses
feeling caricaturish
like one of those
colossal sculptures
of a head
peopled with spleen

peasant revival

scraping together
whatever heritage
I can find
this November
I can really start dressing
I predict a revival
of peasantry
tunics & stockings
hemmed with poverty

*

a day must come
where we die of time
I don't feel like
living longer
fuck mars &
space colonisation
I go down
with this green
down with the borage
& callery pear

*

apropos the impending
the ensuing
the actionable
I'm scheduling a 1-on-1
with the silk hat
of a Bradford

millionaire
apropos his fair
& balanced approach
help will continue
with considerable
constraints

*

say there is a soul
to the nation
imagine it barbed
with anti-homeless spikes
oversharing
its crueltye
remember
there is no such thing
as a synonym

*

there's a waiting
list for the waiting list
to join the community
allotment good job
wild boars were hunted
to extinction
by the 17th century
is it unbelievable
that I want to believe
civic pride
isn't obsolete
that we haven't
murdered
the last sow

rabble

there is a screaming   every other night
   followed by a rumble resembling
        bin day   I don't open the blinds to find
       out whether the noise   is human or boar
weathered as a ghost sign   in my last night's
    dream he escaped from the forest of my old
        home   careening through hedgerows scattering
      passerine spores   behind him a riot
the rabble cast glass and stones at the boar
    glimpsed sharpening his tusks on the trunk
          of a tree as if for conflict   when asked
   why it said   *I do it advisedly*
why sharpen my weapons at the time
     I ought to be using them   the rabble
       assume this means war   the boar is a man
    lying down in the street   what happens
outside is beyond the remit of wonder
        is just another mediated fact

ivegate

everyone knows it as great horton   which is what it is now   *magna*
as in *magna carta*   meaning *great*   I say to my dad in one of the new
coffee shops just off ivegate   it was getting repossessed during the
lockdown no wonder it's charging london prices for mediocre coffee
we're talking about the beck which ran thru the city   still runs   after
the city was rebuilt over it   no longer the lifeblood for fish and power
and water   just something that trickles under the economy above
he's talking about the crossbow killer   how he saw cctv footage of
him assaulting one of his victims   dragging dysstressed by her hair
through the hallway of his flat   a few minutes later she runs out
screaming   he hunts her with a crossbow   shoots her to the floor
after dismembering her   he placed sections of her body in the stream
under the city   we're drinking oat flat whites and looking past each
other   I've heard so much brutality   from an official perspective
how to square it   halloween decorations in the café my mum grew
up in little horton   above *the new house at home*   I wanna taste the
beck   it's brackish water   under the city is a tunnel leading from the
courts to the demolished police station he reckons it's still there   just
walled   off   somewhere   in   wynter   nyght

on the 200th anniversary of the luddite's attack on rawfolds mill

less magpies this year   according
to my dad
yet I have seen
more than dunok or douve
in another life
I would have been a cropper
trimming nap   with these hooves
a carpenter
doing anything   with these hands
save biting to lunula
a luddite   seething
with organisation
after the introduction
of cropping frames   when poor
meant starvation when
hands meant bodies
when synecdoche
meant displacement
across the lost common   a kestrel
hovers against holy wind
I never realised history happens
so close   to home

*

night be night when all
is still & the moon is hid
behind the hill
looking for uber on my phone
I search *luddite*
given the slip by black ice

there is another I beyond
the pale   indebted to time
behind the hill where the moon
crouches in my bed
night chips my teeth

*

tell me   when was the last day
of normal weather
how what the future looks like
depends on who you are
at which tilt you are born
freedom isn't a prerequisite
more commodity
in this economy somebody needs
to personify yvel
male irises
fermented with violence
can you see the devel
scrambling from his bunker
coming for your fields
your forests   and worlds
we forward march to do our will
and strike each haughty tyrant down
with hatchet pike & gun

the new house at home

seen someone else
drivynge yr old car
funny how
inheritance
explodes
into community
yr snub-nosed
genetics
helyxed somewhere
maybe we'd have
got on better
if you still owned
the pub
but the smokynge
ban axed you
like a wunded hog
the parish disbanded
with bad taste
in liquids
upwallen
from sawdust
and yr smoke
machine mouth
the boar emerged
shawled in gore
yarnynge
to anyone near
includynge yr barmaid
turned daughter
how it stalked Cliffe
Wood spookynge

peasants
and townsfolk
until the butcherynge
one outcutten
tongue proffered
to the lord
in exchange
for land and fable
spewed
from the lips
of publicans
milken the bandit
night after night
until 2007
what's a tale
without folk

acknowledgements

Many thanks are due for a research project of this scale. An idea for a project around the Bradford boar folk tale emerged in my thinking early-2020 and gestated through conversations with fellow Bradfordian David Dobson, who read every version of this manuscript.

Thank you to Aaron Kent for publishing this work and having faith in its strangeness.

My endless gratitude to Jasmine Boston, who has commented on early drafts of these poems and gifted amulets of wild boar, in the form of egg cups and charms.

Thanks to Joseph Minden for a kinship of thought and poetics – for his perceptive reading and editorial guidance in the later stages.

Munaza Kulsoom offered some early guidance around Bradford heritage and the image of tongue mutilation in other cultures.

I am grateful to Alex Mepham for their comments on the cover design and engagement with the text.

Thanks to Dom Hale and Tom Crompton from The Poets' Hardship Fund for helping me out during the time of writing.

Lastly, thank you to my sadly-deceased grandad Peter Naylor, who owned the Little House at Home in Little Horton, where folk tales and ghost stories seeped into the fabric of our lives. And to my mum, Julie Branfoot, for her enthusiasm in this book about our geographical heritage.

notes

Most definitions and spellings of Middle English words are from the following sources: the 'Glossary of Dialect' in Mahlham-Dembleby, J. (1912) *Original Tales and Ballads in the Yorkshire Dialect*. London and Felling-on-Tyne: The Walter Scott Publishing Co. Ltd.; Luria, M., and Hoffman, R. L. (1974) *Middle English Lyrics: Authoritative Texts Critical and Historical Backgrounds Perspectives on Six Poems*. New York and London: W. W. Norton.; Stanbury, S. (ed.) (2001) *Pearl*. Michigan: Medieval Institute Publications.

Pages 3-9 rework the received narrative of the Bradford Boar tale as told by Janet C Senior's (n.d.) 'The Legend of the Boar of Bradford' accessed from Bradford Special Collections Library. Janet's website is https://jcs-history.co.uk/.

Italicised quotes in 'church in the woods' are also from Janet C Senior's account. The final line is taken from Collis, S. and Bonney, S. (2015) 'We Are An Other: Poetry, Commons, Subjectivity.' *In* Wah, F. and De'Ath, A. (eds.) *Towards. Some. Air. Remarks on Poetics*. Alberta: Banff Centre Press.

'demesne' was published in Wet Grain, Issue 4, Summer 2023. My gratitude to the editor, Patrick Romero McCafferty and guest editor Sylee Gore.

The title, 'it made sense for the hunter to find out all he could about his quarry', is from Yamamoto, D. (2017) *Wild Boar*. London: Repeater Books, p. 27.

'If the boar feels his tusks are getting blunt, he 'seeketh a herb called *origanum*, and gnaweth it and cheweth it, and cleanest and comforteth the roots of his teeth therewith by virtue thereof" is Yamamoto citing Bartholomaeus Anglicus (pp. 25-26).

'cygnet' cites *Livres du roy Modus et de la royne Racio*, the French hunting manuscript from 1465, equating wild boar with sin, the devil and blackness. It finishes with a line from Edward Topsell's *History of Four-Footed Beasts and Serpents* (1658), both are referencing in Yamamoto (2017 p. 26).

Details of the sacking of the Savoy Palace in 'lost commons' are from Sydney Armitage-Smith's *John of Gaunt* (London, 1904 p. 247).

'I work in a former abattoir' was published by Ink, Sweat and Tears. My gratitude to Chloe Elliott.

The lines 'the silk hat / of a Bradford / millionaire' in 'peasant revival' are from T. S. Eliot's 'The Waste Land' (1922).

'rabble' is inspired by Bhanu Kapil's *Ban en Banlieue* (Nightboat, 2015).

The Bradford Riots happened between 7-9 July 2001, involving confrontation between the British Asian communities in the city and the white population, including far right groups such as the British National Party and the National Front.

The boar and fox is from Aesop's fable as related by Yamamoto (2017 p. 34).

'on the 200th anniversary of the luddite's attack on rawfolds mill' paraphrases lyrics from a folk song about the Luddites called 'The Cropper Lads'.

glossary

Beasts,	cows; cattle.
Beliven,	reamin.
Brass,	coin; money.
Bothrin,	anxiety; worry.
Bovate,	the amount of land tillable by one ox in a ploughing season.
Croodled up,	shrunken up in a heap as with cold or pain.
Cruck house,	a building for peasants or serfs who lived and worked for the manor.
Dreedist,	driest.
Flaysome,	terrible; frightful.
Hip-breear,	wild rose.
Messuage,	a residence, dwelling house; farmstead.
Slaghte,	slaughter or a violent stroke.
Snaht,	snout.
Upwallen,	to emerge from the earth, well up.
Outcutten,	to cut out (the tongue).
Milken,	to milk.
Wacker,	tremble violently.
Wimmin,	women.

LAY OUT YOUR UNREST

We want you to know that the messages you are receiving are indeed real! True! Us!

Yes! You are doing this!

It makes us so happy that we are with you in your heart, that you are feeling our loving guidance! Isn't love just such a wonderful thing?

We have so much more we want to give to you, so much more.

You are doing so well. Isn't this fun?

We love you so much. Today we celebrate.

———— Invocation ————

Angels, please help me feel your loving presence so that I can become more confident in receiving your messages.

Guiding Angels: Guardian Angels

DAY 51

We want you to know that you don't need to take life so seriously.

We want you to know that there can be moments of fun, lightness, softness, laughter, play and joy through every experience.

We want you to know that it is ok to feel happiness and joy as well as sadness in dark times.

We want you to lessen your grip of control on your life.

We want you to know that softness will open you to hear our messages more.

We want you to know that worry blocks you from remembering the possibilities around you.

We want you to remember that life is miraculous every day,

even if just for a moment when you notice a rainbow or smile at a child.

We want you to let this lightness into your being more often.

We want you to allow yourself more time for play. Yes, even more time! Dance! Sing! Laugh!

We want you to let go of the rules. Eat the cake! Follow your dreams. Take the leap of faith. Say yes. Tell someone you love them!

We hope you feel the energy in our message today and smile.

———————— Invocation ————————

Angels, please help me express all aspects of myself, especially those that bring me joy!

Guiding Angels
Archangel Jophiel, Archangel Nathaniel, Archangel Faith

DAY 52

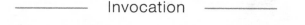
Channelled Angel message

We want you to know that the most beautiful life experiences happen when you least expect it.

We want you to know that the journey of working with us will ask you to let go.

We want you to know that faith is the result of your dialogue with us.

We want you to know that faith creates a pathway for miracles to enter your life, without you even trying.

We want you to know that living in dialogue with us is living in flow with your destiny and highest pathway.

We want you to know that life can be something soft and

gentle, that creation can be a flow rather than a force.

We want you to know that this all comes from letting go.

We want you to know that the energy of this message is for you as well, not just whoever you think is more deserving. This message is for everyone. This message is for you.

We want you to know that there is no special talent or gift required to begin this dialogue. It is as simple as making a decision to begin.

Angels, please help me let go and surrender to the infinite love, guidance, and energy of the divine. Please help me let down my walls so that I can feel at one with the field of creation.

Guiding Angels:
Archangel Uriel, Archangel Faith, Archangel Chamuel

DAY 53

Channelled Angel message

We want you to know that faith creates a softness in your life.

We want you to know that after some time working with us, a gentle thread of faith, peace and calm will begin to emerge.

Some of the tension that has been with you for so long will leave you.

You will notice that you feel lighter, less fearful, more trusting, more patient, more curious, and less attached.

We want you to know that it's ok to let go and soften into your journey of faith. We are here and you are not alone.

We want you to know that faith develops slowly. It is a concept of the mind first, and as you test it out slowly over time, it opens in your heart and never leaves you. Faith grows stronger the more you soften into it.

When you explore the energy of faith, and allow yourself to surrender through your fear barrier, what awaits you is soft.

On the other side of control is a miraculous place. An open place. A playful and joyous place.

Love flows freely to you here, when you surrender and explore faith.

——————— Invocation ———————

Angels, please help me let go and soften into the infinite love of the divine, as I trust and have faith.

Guiding Angels: Archangel Faith, Archangel Michael

DAY 54

Channelled Angel message

We want you to know that when you feel out of sync, this is the discomfort of growth. Things will settle soon.

Some days will feel uncomfortable.

Some days, you may notice that you feel out of alignment.

Some days, everything around you may be in a state of flux or may feel so.

We want you to know that this is what it feels like when you are learning to live and see in a new way; when you are practising a new approach, when you are letting go of old patterns that you have identified no longer work for you.

Discomfort is sometimes a part of life and it's ok.

We are here to support you through the in-between time, as you get used to a new situation.

We can guide you to practices that will help anchor your new choices and ground you when you feel unsettled.

We also want you to know that you are doing great, and it's ok to have days that feel uncomfortable. This shows you are growing and changing. We are so proud of the work you are doing!

—————— Invocation ——————

Angels, please help me be patient as I experience the discomfort of growth and change. Please remind me that this will pass. Please show me the path that is in alignment with my highest timeline.

Guiding Angels:
Archangel Nathaniel, Archangel Faith, Archangel Michael

DAY 55

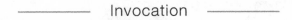

Channelled Angel message

We want you to know that it is ok to give yourself space and time now. There is no rush.

We want you to know that there is really no need for you to know the outcome right now.

We want you to remember that things are playing out to a timeline of divine perfection for all involved.

We want you to remember to practise faith and let go now.

We want you to remember that making decisions is sometimes a way that you will block miracles. How can miracles flow to you if you do not have faith and create space for them?

We want you to know that things that are removed from your life are removed to make space for something better.

We want you to have faith that there is a big picture here that you do not fully understand.

Step back. Get busy elsewhere. Give your energy to the things that flow easily, to the people that love you with the same amount of love that you give them, to the activities and projects that light a fire inside you!

Give yourself a little space and time. What you can see as possible right now is only the tip of the iceberg, and with patience, other pathways will emerge.

We see so much possibility around you right now. Can you have faith, step back, and allow it to manifest into reality?

Invocation

Angels, please assist me to step back and let go of the need to take action now from a place of fear or control. Please help me remember that there are miracles that await me in the not knowing, and that I am worthy of receiving them.

Guiding Angels:
Archangel Faith, Archangel Ariel, Archangel Jophiel

DAY 56

Channelled Angel message

We want you to know that it will feel uncomfortable growing into yourself, but we will be there with you.

This is part of your purpose.

All you need to do is follow your heart and do the things you love, and everything will fall into place.

It won't be easy. It won't be perfect. You will still have challenges like everyone else.

We want you to know that as you let go, you become more you.

We want you to know that with letting go comes faith.

We want you to know that as you grow, everything will feel different. This can feel uncomfortable.

We want you to know that the rewards for you here are limitless.

We want to help you through the transition periods, to guide you with ways to grow through the discomfort.

We want you to continue this open curiosity you are bringing to your relationship with us. We want you to continue this open curiosity that you are bringing to all your relationships, and to your relationship with yourself.

—— Invocation ——

Angels, please help me begin to let go and become curious now. Please assist me through the discomfort of this awakening period.

Guiding Angels:
Archangel Haniel, Archangel Michael, Archangel Faith

DAY 57

Channelled Angel message

There is a new energy on Earth. This energy is light. We see that some of you call this the 5D energy.

We see this energy as light. There is now more light on Earth than ever before.

Being human will feel different to how it has ever felt before. To how it did last year. To how it did last month.

Your understanding of what is possible, of healing, of time, of creation and of consciousness is all coming into question. This is because it all feels different to you. This is because you feel more light around you.

The light makes it easier to heal.

The light means change and transformation can happen more easily, more quickly.

The light means that miracles can happen more easily.

The light means that you can hear us more easily.

It will feel uncomfortable at times as you adjust and acclimatise to the new energy.

This new energy will trigger growth and healing for those who are ready.

You do not need to do this alone. We are here to support you.

You are not alone in feeling like everything is different. Many feel this.

Invocation

Angels, please help me as I begin to adjust to and awaken to receive greater light and love in my being.

Guiding Angels:
Archangel Metatron, Archangel Chamuel, Archangel Jophiel

DAY 58

Channelled Angel message

We want you to know that if you spend more time in nature, you can adjust more easily to the new Earth energies.

We want you to know that you are supported energetically by Earth and by nature more than you understand.

We want you to know that you are in energetic circuitry with the earth.

We want you to know that spending time in nature and with

your body touching the earth has powerful positive effects.

We want you to know that you are highly sensitive and that when you feel out of sorts, spending time connected to the earth can rebalance you.

We want you to know that as the energies on Earth shift and change, so you will shift and change, and that the easiest way to adjust is by being in nature.

We want you to open to this idea of your energy being in constant energetic circuitry with the earth.

We want you to imagine a pillar of light connecting from the centre of the earth, through you, to the heavens.

This is how we see you. This is your light footprint.

We want you to recall that you can be fully recharged physically and energetically by the earth.

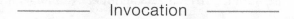

Invocation

Angels, please remind me daily to spend time with my body on the earth so that I can come into harmonic attunement with the earth's frequency.

Guiding Angels:
Archangel Gaia, Archangel Gersisa, Archangel Metatron

DAY 59

Channelled Angel message

We invite you to start making decisions with love as your guide.

We invite you to be curious about fear and notice where it has been guiding you until now.

We invite you to get curious about faith as part of this process.

We know that deep down this message feels like the way you

have always wanted to live.

We invite you to work with us as you play with this process.

We invite you to make it fun, joyous, and rebellious.

We invite you to get to know your passions as you explore love guiding you.

We invite you to soften into love, knowing we are with you, and that you are safe and held here.

—————— Invocation ——————

Angels, please show me the pathway of love, joy, passion, and play. Please help me walk through my fears and walls to unlock this pathway.

Guiding Angels:
Archangel Jophiel, Archangel Chamuel, Archangel Michael

DAY 60

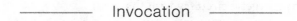

We want you to know that it's ok to not know the answer. You will one day.

We invite you to be gentle and loving with yourself when you are growing.

As you explore, be curious, stretch and play with your life, at times you will be unsure.

Everything happens for a reason.

There are no mistakes in life.

Everything teaches you something.

You won't always know what to do, or how things will turn out.

We applaud you for stepping in anyway.

We are with you, and the discomfort you feel in the 'not knowing' will settle soon.

This time you are moving through will be a memory one day, and we want you to allow some of our love in now to ease any discomfort you feel.

―――――――― Invocation ――――――――

Angels, please help me be patient while I wait for clarity. Please show me my next step and highest pathway.

Guiding Angels:
Archangel Haniel, Archangel Chamuel, Archangel Michael

DAY 61

Angel lesson: Archangel Jophiel

Archangel Jophiel brings positivity, joy, happiness, self-love, self-worth, and radiance into your life.

Archangel Jophiel has a feminine energy and deep-pink aura with a bright white centre.

She wants to help you bring the feelings of positive energy, love, self-worth, radiance, beauty, and body love into your being.

She sees that this is within you and ready to be expressed.

She knows that you are craving this feeling within you, and she wants you to know that you can work with her to bring more positivity into your life.

She wants you to know that your heart will expand with confidence and joy as you begin to love yourself and your life more during the process of working with her.

She invites you to immerse yourself in her energy and support and love.

She will work with you for as long as it takes and as long as you need.

──────── Invocation ────────

Archangel Jophiel, I invite you to work with me now. Please help me remember my worth and grow into my true self.

Guiding Angel: Archangel Jophiel
Energy: Feminine
Aura colour: Deep/bright pink

DAY 62

Channelled Angel message

We want you to know that relationships are a big part of the purpose of life. And that love is in all relationships.

We invite you to open to shifting your understanding of relationships.

We invite you to look at love as the reason for all experiences.

We want you to see that even difficult experiences contain opportunities to express love, receive love, and learn about love.

We want you to know that you exist in relationship, in connection. Always.

We want you to know that all relationships are sacred and exist in divine perfection. All relationships help you learn about and experience love.

We want you to know that even fleeting connections have a purpose. The stranger who smiles at you has a purpose. The stranger who expresses anger to you has a purpose.

We want you to open to exploring how you can give and receive more love in all your relationships. Including, and perhaps most importantly, your relationship with yourself.

Love is all around you once you open to it. It is within you once you remember it. It can explode in your life once you recall that it's ok to feel the full spectrum of love.

Love is grief. Love is pain. Love is joy. Love is ecstasy. Love is sadness. Love is laughter. Love is softness. Love is anger. Love exists in every moment, not just in the romantic and positive ones.

We invite you to begin to open and soften to explore and experience love.

Invocation

Angels, please help me let go of control in relationships, so that I can be present to the full gifts of the experience.

Guiding Angels:
Archangel Chamuel, Archangel Raguel, Archangel Zadkiel

DAY 63

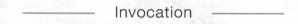

Channelled Angel message

We want you to know that when you work with us, things feel softer.

We invite you to remember that we agreed to support you before you were born.

We invite you to remember the feeling of love that awaits you when you eventually return to the light.

We invite you to remember that from where we sit, there is no better-than or worse-than experience on Earth. They are all miracles. Do you remember this? Do you remember choosing all the shades of your human life?

We invite you to remember that there is a love that is so vast and expansive that your human heart barely comprehends it. When it does, it's in glimpses that make everything worthwhile.

We invite you to remember that this love exists always, and that you can recall it, and feel it more often when you work with us.

We invite you to soften into these messages and recall your divinity and find faith.

—————— Invocation ——————

Angels, please remind me that I am safe to soften and awaken to the infinite love of the divine now.

Guiding Angels:
Guardian Angels, Archangel Faith, Archangel Michael

DAY 64

Channelled Angel message

We want you to know that from our perspective, there is no bad experience. No worse-than experience. There are only experiences. All have value.

We want you to see that life has a different purpose from what you may believe.

We want you to see that all humans experience pain and suffering.

We want you to know that there is meaning in all experiences.

We want you to know that no human has it better than you. We invite you to stop comparing your experience and shift your focus to understanding and accepting your experience.

We invite you to let go of placing value on your worth because of your experience.

We know that this might feel hard, and we want you to know that the pathway to surrender is via faith.

We invite you to let go. Categorising or judging your experience prolongs your pain and prevents you from seeing the pathway presenting to you in this moment.

There is love here for you.

It has always been here.

You will find it when you are ready.

You have not done anything to deserve your experience. By that thinking, all humans are being punished. Or rewarded. Life is not like that. That logic does not work when all humans experience both joy and suffering.

We invite you to play with these concepts, be curious, explore them, and open to them.

We invite you to feel our loving acceptance of you. And notice that you feel lighter, more peaceful, more accepting of yourself when you work with us.

——————— Invocation ———————

Angels, please help me let go of judgement and comparison. Please help me trust that the experience I am having is leading me to the life that I desire.

Guiding Angels: Guardian Angels, Archangel Zadkiel

DAY 65

Channelled Angel message

We want you to know that we love you no matter what. We see your full potential. We see the things you think are unlovable. And we love you.

We want you to know that there is nothing you need to do to deserve our love.

We want you to know that there is nothing you could do that would stop us loving you.

We want you to know that we love you unconditionally.

We want you to practise opening your heart to the awareness of unconditional love, as it will help you feel our loving presence.

We want you to be aware of where you can love yourself unconditionally.

We want you to be aware of where you can love others unconditionally.

We want you to be curious and explore love, both in giving and receiving.

We hope you see this begins with knowing, with faith, that we will always, always love you.

———— Invocation ————

Angels, please help me open to unconditional love. Please help me first feel and explore this with you so that I can then explore it within my own heart.

Guiding Angels: Archangel Chamuel

DAY 66

Channelled Angel message

We invite you to practise unconditional love and see how your life transforms.

We invite you to be curious, playful, and open to this as a journey, an exploration.

We invite you to notice that this practice begins with yourself.

We invite you to open to the idea that it extends to all living beings, not just romantic love.

We invite you to notice that when you explore this idea, you detach, and feel space around you.

We invite you to notice that unconditional love is soft. That it is accepting. That it is warm, loving and kind.

We invite you to explore the idea that you can still have boundaries and love unconditionally.

We invite you to notice that the key awareness is acceptance and detachment.

This is another aspect of love. Do you remember this feeling? It exists in your energy field and in your heart. You come from this love. You return to this love. You ARE this love.

───────── Invocation ─────────

Angels, please show me the pathway to loving unconditionally.

Guiding Angels: Archangel Chamuel

DAY 67

Channelled Angel message

We want you to know that nothing is set in stone. All future possibilities exist. What is meant to be will come exactly when it is meant to.

Time does not exist.

Energy is swirling all around you, and you are interacting with the energy of all possible outcomes at all times.

The divine works in your favour.

The divine interacts with all.

The outcome that eventuates is divine perfection for all

involved.

The outcome that eventuates comes in perfect timing.

Everything is perfection because it is.

There is nothing you need to do. What will be will be, at the exact divinely perfect moment.

You can let it float to you in divine timing.

And you are not alone in the in-between, not-knowing, alchemical becoming of what will be.

You are infinitely loved by us. By the universe. By God.

─────── Invocation ───────

Angels, please help me let go of attachment to linear time and all outcomes so that I may flow and receive in perfect divine timing.

Guiding Angels: Archangel Faith, Guardian Angels

DAY 68

Channelled Angel message

We want you to know that your choices change the future. You can create a whole new timeline in an instant.

We want you to know that sometimes you will feel stuck or blocked for a long time, and then when you are ready, everything will seem to change.

We want you to know that your ideas about what is possible have an impact on what is actually possible.

We want you to open to this message, and see that when your beliefs change, your choices and actions change.

There is magic in this creation process.

The divine is connecting with you in every moment.

There is perfection in your timing. Your choices and actions are creation in motion; your actions are creating energetic ripples in time and space in every moment.

You are one with the divine, as are all living beings, for you are the divine expressing itself through you.

Everything exists in perfect state as is.

You will feel uncomfortable as you begin to create a new pathway and timeline. Your physical and energetic body will respond to the new energy being created. This will feel different. Of course, it will! It's new! You have never felt it before.

We want you to know that the power and worth you require to begin creating a new pathway that aligns with your highest good exist now in this moment.

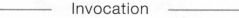

Invocation

Angels, please help me remember my infinite power to create and express through my consciousness.

Guiding Angels:
Archangel Ariel, Archangel Metatron, Archangel Uriel

DAY 69

Channelled Angel message

We want you to know that life is like a series of lots of small steps.

We want you to know that knowing the final outcome is not always in your best interests.

We want you to know that sometimes we will answer your question about the future by redirecting your focus to the place that is most important for you right now—the place that will create a future you have not even realised is possible.

We want you to know that the end result is never set in stone and can change at any given moment due to the free will of all involved.

We want you to know that there is always immediate guidance available to you to help you on your next step.

We want you to see that focusing too far ahead can distract you from the experience of right now.

We want you to know that whilst we might give you glimpses of how the future might feel, this is still only one possible outcome of many. Your choice, and the choices of others, can still change the outcome.

We want you to bring your focus into now, into how you feel in your heart right now.

We want you to see that as you take small steps, you create big change.

———————— Invocation ————————

Angels, please help me let go and experience this moment with curiosity, love and peace.

Guiding Angels: Archangel Chamuel

DAY 70

Channelled Angel message

When you feel afraid, confused, or unsure, we invite you to get curious. What is the spiritual purpose of this experience? How can we assist you?

We have said before, everything happens for a reason.

This is true both on an individual and collective level. And both are connected.

We invite you to notice fear and get curious.

We invite you to notice when you feel confused and look for clarity.

We invite you to notice when you feel alone or disconnected and ask for our support. You do not need to experience your most challenging moments alone. We are here to offer love, support, and guidance.

We want to remind you that when you feel afraid, it is a starting point on your journey to that which you desire. We invite you to become curious and hopeful—excited about growth and change.

When you feel uncertain and unsure, we invite you to look in different directions for answers you may not see yet. We invite you to look around you at what you already have and refocus there. This is often an opportunity to gain perspective and clarity. We can assist you.

We invite you to step back a little. To look at things with a lens of curiosity. To practise faith and remember that you are ok. You are safe. You are not alone. You are loved.

———— Invocation ————

Angels, please show me what I can't see.

Guiding Angels: Archangel Haniel

DAY 71

Channelled Angel message

We invite you to take life less seriously. To look at situations as an opportunity to practise.

We invite you to embrace life with joy, wonder, and carefree curiosity!

We invite you to be playful, light-hearted and inquisitive!

We hope you can open to see that blocks, wrong turns and 'mistakes' are ok, and part of the experience, and that often they are gateways, right turns, and perfect choices.

We hope you can take life less seriously and know that there is always time to make changes.

We invite you to see how fun life can be!

We would like you to open to possibilities that seem risky, scary, rebellious, or courageous.

We invite you to let yourself dream, hope, and explore!

There really are no mistakes. Every experience has a purpose, and we invite you to let go a little on your journey.

Invocation

Angels, please help me soften into a playful and curious exploration of life now.

Guiding Angels: Archangel Jophiel

DAY 72

Angel lesson: Archangel Uriel

Archangel Uriel helps you reconnect with the divine, remember your oneness, and heal your relationship with God.

Archangel Uriel wants you to know that Angels are not religious.

Archangel Uriel wants you to allow yourself to forgive and heal any pain you have in your relationship with God.

Archangel Uriel wants you to allow yourself to be supported by the divine, by the Angels, by God.

Archangel Uriel wants you to know that the love and support of the divine is there right now. You are connected to it even if you are unaware.

Archangel Uriel asks you to spend time in the sunshine, to receive the energy of the sun and to connect with him in that energy.

Archangel Uriel explains that the sunshine clears your vibration and realigns you with the energy of the divine.

Archangel Uriel invites you to work with him. His aura is soft golden yellow. He feels comforting, reassuring, safe and empowering. You feel worthy and loved when you connect with him.

―――――― Invocation ――――――

Archangel Uriel, I invite you to work with me now. Please help me open to healing my relationship with God and remember that I am one with all living beings. Please help me gently open to the light of source and receive the love that I am in fact connected to.

Guiding Angel: Archangel Uriel
Energy: Masculine
Aura colour: Yellow

DAY 73

Channelled Angel message

We want you to know that there really is nothing to fear.

If you feel afraid, we invite you to work with Archangel Michael.

From where we sit, you are safe and loved.

From where we sit, when you feel afraid, you become disconnected momentarily from the divine.

We invite you to spend time in nature when you feel

disconnected from source, from the divine, from unconditional love.

We invite you to speak with us when you feel disconnected from love.

We invite you to bring our loving guidance into your energy when you feel overcome with the energy of fear.

We can assist you. We love you!

There is nothing to fear. You are safe and all is well.

———— Invocation ————

Angels, please help me feel safe, connected,
and loved in this moment.

Guiding Angels: Archangel Michael

DAY 74

Channelled Angel message

We want you to know that things are different now.

That's why we are here.

It's not your imagination.

This is a very significant time of change for you, and for all humans.

You chose to be here now, to be a part of this change.

You do not need to do this alone. We can support you.

This is an important experience.

You do have a role to play.

Your feelings are guiding you correctly.

Love is the way forward.

Things feel like they are breaking around you. Yes. We know. They are and this will continue.

This time is destined, and we chose to come through now to assist this process.

You are a part of this. Everyone is.

Invocation

Angels, please help me through the process of awakening to infinite love now. Please help me process and open to the change as it presents for me.

Guiding Angels:
Archangel Haniel, Archangel Metatron, Archangel Michael

DAY 75

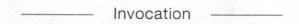

Channelled Angel message

There is always love when you look for it.

We want to speak with you about the message that everything happens for a reason.

We want to help you find the spiritual purpose for your experience, and to ease the pain or suffering you might be feeling.

We invite you to become curious when you are experiencing pain, discomfort, worry or sadness, or feeling afraid.

We invite you to look for love.

There is always love in your life, and this exploration is the gateway to understanding your experience.

It is the way to faith, and to reconnection to the divine.

It is the way to access the love that is your birthright and all around you, always.

We love you. We can help you find love when you feel disconnected.

Go to nature. We will find you there.

Angels, please help me awaken now to the perfection in my experience and find the pathway of love.

Guiding Angels:
Archangel Haniel, Archangel Faith, Archangel Chamuel

DAY 76

Angel lesson: Archangel Faith

Archangel Faith assists us with the spiritual journey of faith, feeling safe deepening our relationship with the divine, and trusting our intuitive guidance.

Archangel Faith has an instantly calming and peaceful energy. She radiates safety, reassurance, confidence, and resilience. She feels grounding, affirming and gentle when we connect with her, and all our fears of the unknown dissipate when we work with her.

Archangel Faith is working with us now as we journey through the veil and begin to collectively open our natural intuitive gifts to connect with the non-physical, with the divine, with the Angelic realms, and with miracles.

Archangel Faith helps us connect with our inner guidance, and the journey of awakening to our sovereign ability to deepen our powerful intuitive gifts. She helps allay any fears that come up as we unlock from programming, limiting beliefs, and past lives where using our intuition has resulted in danger, trauma, persecution, and death.

Archangel Faith helps us heal our relationship with the divine in all forms, and let go of all our blocks, walls, beliefs, and veils which we have created as protection mechanisms, which are in the way of being in infinite flow with the source of all creation.

Archangel Faith is present when we are moving through times of rapid spiritual development, change and growth. We can call on her when we do not see out next steps and are waiting for divine timing to bring us clarity and the path forwards. She helps us let go and find peace with the miraculous process of life, and to open to trust the divine.

——————— Invocation ———————

Archangel Faith, I invite you to work with me now. Please help me feel safe opening to the unknown, to the divine, to change, and to let go of control. Please help me trust that I am safe to follow my intuition and have faith in my own heart guidance.

Guiding Angels: Archangel Faith
Energy: Feminine
Aura colour: Pastel green and pink

DAY 77

Channelled Angel message

We want you to know that even when it seems like everything is crumbling around you, there is still love. Joy. Hope.

We are closer to you than ever before.

We are surrounding you with love to balance the fear that you feel.

We want you to see that there is a pathway through your current experience.

We want you to feel the massive love that exists—it is so huge! It is within you, around you, in us, in your family, in your friends, in all humans, in all living beings. It is in music, in nature, in laughter, in play, in art, in the sunshine, in the clouds, in the rain, in flowers, in rainbows, in kisses.

When you feel disconnected, when you see things breaking or changing around you, we remind you to look also at that which is growing. That which is love. That which is miraculous. That which is spontaneity, compassion, kindness.

This is a miracle unfolding right now.

------- Invocation -------

Angels, please assist me when I feel fear to see another perspective: that which is love.

Guiding Angels:
Archangel Michael, Archangel Nathaniel, Archangel Chamuel

DAY 78

Channelled Angel message

We want you to know that practising detachment will change everything for you.

We invite you to remember that you have no control of the external, only your own perception.

Alongside this, we invite you to trust that everything will work out exactly as it's supposed to, and that you will be ok. Please allow yourself to close your eyes and feel this message with your heart.

Now we invite you to feel how supported and loved you are by the divine, by us, by the earth and all plants and animals. Notice how literally everything that exists does so to support you, to support life. Notice and recall that you are connected to every living thing. That you are magnificent, powerful, and loved unconditionally. That you are a living manifestation of love.

Now we invite you to notice the space that opens up around you when you explore this. Do you see how things begin to soften? How your heart expands and you expand into a bit more of your radiant magnificence? How joy flows through you and love settles in and calms those fears?

We want you to practise detachment as a gateway to love, to faith, to us and to all that you desire.

─────────── Invocation ───────────

Angels, please help me surrender, let go, and open to the infinite love and support of the divine as expressed as all life.

Guiding Angels:
Archangel Uriel, Archangel Faith, Archangel Michael

DAY 79

Channelled Angel message

When you see disruption, death, uncertainty, we see creation, birth, destiny.

We want you to know that there is a significant experience unfolding right now for the collective.

We want you to know that it is not all as it seems.

We invite you to detach and work with us.

We invite you to become curious and let your heart guide you through this experience.

The journey now is imperative to the evolution of humanity. And your journey is also crucial to the collective experience.

Love must guide you now, more than ever before. We bring urgency to the need to let your heart guide you forward.

We call on you to step into service if that is your pathway. This is a time of activation for all light workers and starseeds (these terms are not ours; we know you understand the meaning).

Your mission contract is being activated now.

We invite you to step into your heart and detach from the collective fear. Your pathway is to create a new world, internally and externally. You are ready for this. You chose to incarnate now to be a part of this collective shift.

There is more creation force available to you now than ever before.

There is more light available on Earth than ever before.

There is more love present than ever before.

Look for the love. Look for the humour. Look for the creativity, genius and new pathways birthing now. And become a leader, a wayshower of this new time of creation.

A new world is coming. You are a part of this.

Your new inner world is blossoming and opening now in readiness.

The two are connected.

───────── Invocation ─────────

Angels, please assist me to step into clarity about my mission now. Please help me begin to see my pathway through this time of change.

Guiding Angels: Archangel Haniel, Archangel Michael

DAY 80

Channelled Angel message

We want you to know that you chose to be here now.

We want you to know that whatever your experience is today, now, it's not a coincidence.

Every pathway and every thread has connected you here now.

Every person in your life is there for a reason.

You are in theirs for a reason too.

The collective experience is part of your journey.

You contribute to the collective experience too.

Magic is occurring now. Magic occurs every day, but you can feel it now, can't you?

Sometimes your destiny steps in, and you see all the threads leading up to a certain point. This is one of those moments.

Sometimes you see everything around you with a new perspective. This is one of those moments.

We are here to assist you through this incredible expansion, individually and collectively. That's why we are here now.

We are always here. Right here. Waiting to assist you.

─────────── Invocation ───────────

Angels, please help me remember the magical creation energy that exists always, in me and around me.

Guiding Angels: Archangel Ariel, Archangel Faith

DAY 81

Channelled Angel message

When you are in the light, in the vibration of love, you become a beacon. A lighthouse.

We wish to remind you of a spiritual truth today. When there is tremendous fear, we remind you that light and love can clear that instantly.

In order to dissipate fear, we remind you to come back into love. To do the things that bring you back into the light and back into the vibration of love.

We remind you that when you are in the light, and in the energy of love, this emanates and radiates from you!

Your energy and vibration are more powerful than you can ever realise!

For some of you—those who are ready and have been called to service—your light heals others. Your light activates others. Your light awakens others.

Your light is needed now.

There are many processing fear as the collective shifts and awakens.

There are many awakening.

There are many who are confused and afraid.

If you are not afraid, if you are in your light, if you have a soul contract to serve now, we invite you to work with us.

We remind you of the truth that your love, your light, is needed now.

We remind you that light and love shine the way through this experience.

We remind you that light and love have always been the way.

We remind you that you are made of light and love.

We remind you that light and love bring acceptance to all fear, and a pathway to healing.

We remind you to urgently step into your purpose, which is activating now.

──────── Invocation ────────

Angels, please help me find the love and light within my own heart, so that I may become a radiant beacon of light for all those I come into contact with.

Guiding Angels: Archangel Metatron, Archangel Michael

DAY 82

Channelled Angel message

We invite you to trust your heart and your intuition now more than ever.

We want you to know that the experience you are moving through right now is one that you are ready for.

We want you to know that every moment of every day, you can feel your way through this experience with your heart and your intuition.

This does not mean that you do not also use your logic and mind.

However, many of you are unfamiliar with using your heart and your intuition to the same degree, and in balance.

We want you to notice where you are disconnected from your heart or repressing feelings. This is the pathway to explore now.

We invite you to work with us to become curious, and notice where your life now feels different, what perspective you now have as things change around you, and how your heart feels as you awaken.

We invite you to notice that you do indeed know the answers. That you do indeed know your own personal truth.

As your life changes rapidly around you, we invite you to let your heart lead now. What do you love? Who do you love? How can you express more of yourself? How can you be more you?

———————— Invocation ————————

Angels, please help me open my heart, trust my heart guidance, and feel safe expressing my feelings now.

Guiding Angels:
Archangel Chamuel, Archangel Raphael, Archangel Zadkiel

DAY 83

Channelled Angel message

We want you to know that faith is not about religion. And that we are not about religion.

We will repeat this message many times.

We see you experiencing turbulence and lack of peace.

We see fear and disconnection.

We love you. We invite you to know that we do not judge you for feeling disconnected or afraid. And we invite you to practise compassion towards yourself. This is very human.

We also invite you to work with us!

We invite you to allow our loving guidance and support to assist you as you navigate all your life experiences, not just the challenging ones.

We want you to know that it is ok to let go, and open to receive our support.

We invite you to notice where you are struggling alone.

We invite you to soften and open to the loving guidance of the divine.

We invite you to take a leap of faith ... and open to our messages.

We want you to know that there is nothing that is unsafe about working with us.

We want you to know that you were always able to work with us, and that now is a collective time of remembering this.

——————— Invocation ———————

Angels, please remind me that I already know my Angels. Please help me remember that I am safe to open to the divine now.

Guiding Angels:
Archangel Uriel, Archangel Haniel, Archangel Michael

DAY 84

Channelled Angel message

We want you to know that there is no perfect outcome. There never has been.

We remind you that there is a divine order to everything.

Whatever outcome occurs is exactly what is needed for the soul contracts of you, and all involved.

In this sense, we invite you to open to the idea that perfection is a belief. And that by attaching meaning to an outcome that you believe to be the one you require, you create limits and expectation, which disconnects you from the experience that is unfolding around you.

Life is more about the journey and experience.

The miracles exist in the space where you detach from the outcome.

When we work with you, we will only ever give you glimpses, hints of possible outcomes, so that you can make choices that feel right to you.

Nothing is ever set in stone.

You have free will, as do all humans.

We invite you to soften and open into this message today—to know that there is an experience here for you. Even in suffering.

We understand that it's tempting to make meaning of 'good' and 'bad' experiences and outcomes.

And again, we remind you that all are a part of the plan and the journey.

Practising peace with this concept will open you up to the energy of creation, of manifestation, and of miracles.

Non-attachment is a key part of this message and leads you to faith.

And faith is found in acceptance of what is and trust in the infinite love of the divine.

Faith as an energy allows you to be open to all possible outcomes. Attachment limits this process.

--------- Invocation ---------

Angels, please help me practise detachment and faith in this moment.

Guiding Angels: Archangel Faith, Archangel Michael

DAY 85

Channelled Angel message

We want you to know that there are powerful forces of love working in your favour. Now and always.

We want you to know that every single event that occurs in your life is always considered, guided, orchestrated, and created with divine perfection for all beings.

Even now.

There is so much light and love flooding Earth right now. If you could only see it!

There are beams of light pouring into Earth to support the current vibrational shifts, to anchor more light into your home that you call Earth, or Gaia.

The light frequency is rising rapidly.

As this occurs, you experience a response, a shift in awareness. All humans do.

This is a process of love.

Love supports you and all living beings now. The divine supports you and all living beings.

There is a collective and an individual experience. Both are connected.

Every single experience has meaning and importance.

Your individual experience is vital.

Love is the way forward, and through.

If you can close your eyes, for a moment, and imagine love that creates immense beams of light pouring down from the heavens now, this is just a fraction of the magnificence of the divine support flooding Earth now. This love and support is available to you.

Many of you feel it, and rather than feeling afraid now, you feel faith, peace, joy!

We want you to know that you are surrounded by love.

───────────── Invocation ─────────────

Angels, please remind me of the infinite love within me, and around me. Please remind me that I am one with this infinite source of love.

Guardian Angels: Archangel Chamuel

DAY 86

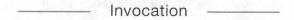

Channelled Angel message

We want you to know that you have never needed to spiritually protect yourself.

We want you to know that it's just about remembering your power. This is recalled when you bring light into your being.

We want you to know that the light is the vibration of love.

We want you to know that whenever you feel out of alignment, afraid or unsafe, or in need of protection, all you need to do is bring more light into your being.

When you access the light and fuel your body with love, there is no need for temporary spiritual protection.

Many of you will understand this process as raising your vibration.

We see it as using the light as fuel. Using love as energy.

The quickest way to return to the light is in nature.

There has never been a more important time to allow your body to contact the earth, even if for a short time.

If you are unable to do this, being in sunshine is also powerful.

If you are unable to do this, there are many other activities and actions that bring light. Choose any action that feels like love.

We leave you with a visual of a pillar of light pouring down from the heavens around you at all times. That is all you need to imagine, and it is so. As you raise your vibration, there is no longer a need for protection, for you recall your power in that moment.

————— Invocation —————

Angels, please surround me with a pillar of infinite source light, so that I may easily and quickly clear and expand my frequency to its maximum level in this moment.

Guiding Angels:
Archangel Michael, Archangel Metatron, Archangel Butyalil

DAY 87

Channelled Angel message

Today we will speak to you about the current global experience.

This is both a collective and individual frequency shift. This is a major shift that was destined to occur now. You chose to be here now.

This is a time when all that was hidden will become visible.

On an individual level, you will experience new awareness as you discover your own shadows.

On a collective level, you will also experience shifts in perception and awareness.

This may be experienced as revelations, or disclosure, whether as part of your internal or external process.

There is nothing to fear. This is the journey of enlightenment.

This is not a bad experience. There is no 'bad' experience. It is just another experience.

There are so many miracles unfolding right now; we encourage you to stay curious, open, and detached from the meaning around the collective journey.

We encourage you to spend time with your body on the earth now, to balance the frantic and electric energy that is sometimes present in the collective.

The light can assist you now. We are sending pillars of light to surround you.

Please be in nature, and in sunshine, as much as you are able to right now.

Please use your light practice more than ever now.

—————— Invocation ——————

Angels, please surround me in light and show me
all that I cannot see.

Guiding Angels:
Archangel Michael, Archangel Metatron, Archangel Haniel

DAY 88

Angel lesson: Archangel Sandalphon

Archangel Sandalphon can help you hear your Angel messages, and express or explore the light via creative expression, including music and poetry.

Archangel Sandalphon's energy is uplifting, joyful, heart opening, and loving.

He works with all poets and musicians and anyone who wants to receive downloads of musical or poetic inspiration.

He helps your connection to the divine when it comes to sending and receiving messages with Angels and with God.

He wants you to know that music is a form of healing, and that its vibration is of God, of love, of the universe, of source.

He wants you to know that music is very important always, but especially now, as a vibrational balance to the lower frequencies and fear energy.

He wants you to know that everyone can work with him, and everyone can benefit from music, poetry and the wonderful creative expression of marvellous humans now. That this is an expression of love, of creation, of the divine, and will lift your vibration and open your heart to the divine now.

--------- Invocation ---------

Archangel Sandalphon, I invite you to work with me now.
Please help me connect to the divine creation force to receive
and channel music and poetic inspiration. Please facilitate clear
communication between myself and the divine.

Guiding Angel: Archangel Sandalphon
Energy: Masculine
Aura colour: Turquoise

DAY 89

Channelled Angel message

We want you to know that it's ok to take life a little less seriously.

We want you to know that with this, there really are no rules. Most rules are made up by humans.

We want you to know that all parts of your experience are valuable.

We want you to know that you can make up your own life rules when it comes to your experience and your passions.

We want you to know that we do not judge you for any of your choices.

In fact, we love seeing the diversity, creativity, and expression of humans! We love seeing you happy.

If you love to dress a particular way that is not common, we encourage you to do what makes you feel happy.

If you feel happy eating meat, we support you.

If eating a vegan diet makes you feel joyful and energised, we encourage and support you!

If you love heavy metal music, we are happy!

If you love to pole dance, we applaud you!

We do not hold judgement over your choices.

We invite you to notice when you are shrinking, restricting, or hiding parts of yourself.

We invite you to notice where your beliefs are changing. Be curious. Is this feeling joyful to you? Or are you shrinking to fit in?

We invite you to notice that perceptions are under the spotlight for the collective now, when they become beliefs, rules, and judgements.

We invite you to detach and take some time to explore what really feels like your pathway, your beliefs, your joy, your passion.

Angels, please help me detach from needing to fit in, and express myself authentically as I feel guided by my heart.

Guiding Angels:
Archangel Nathaniel, Archangel Jophiel, Archangel Michael

DAY 90

Channelled Angel message

We want you to know that you can access our loving guidance anywhere, instantly.

We want you to know that you can speak to us in your mind, even when you are in a crowded location, and we hear you. Always.

We want you to know that there are no rituals required to speak with us. There is no gift for a select few. This is something you can learn to do. Everyone can remember/learn to speak with Angels.

We want you to know that when you feel disconnected, afraid, lonely or sad, all you need to do is call for us, and we can flood you with light and love from source.

We want you to know that you don't need to be religious to work with us. We are not religion. We are love!

We want you to know that we will not always answer your question the way you expect. Some things you are meant to experience. We will not give away the outcome, as that is against all spiritual laws (and not in your highest good). We will always guide you in a way that is loving and supportive.

We always have guidance available for you.

We always have love available for you.

We will never judge you.

We accept you exactly as you are.

*Angels, please remind me that you are with me in every moment,
and that I can call on you whenever I need, as often as I need.*

Guiding Angels:
Guardian Angels, Archangel Uriel, Archangel Sandalphon

DAY 91

Channelled Angel message

We want you to know that everything is ok.

We want you to know that even though there is great change occurring around you right now, you are ok.

We want you to know that change is always occurring.

We want you to know that uncertainty is always present.

We want you to know that you are far stronger than you realise, and that you are able to cope and manage through this experience.

We want you to let go of worries about the future and soften into faith.

We want you to practise curiously exploring your current experience, asking questions, noticing new perceptions and awareness.

We want you to know that there is a reason for everything, for every individual, and for the collective.

We want you to know that the experience you have right now is neither good nor bad. It is just another experience.

We want you to know that light, love, joy, growth, learning, peace, and many other wonderful aspects of life exist right now, as they always do.

We want you to practise compassion and self-love on days when you do not feel happy. Unhappiness is part of life, and you are safe to explore and express your feelings.

We want you to know that this is a wonderful experience, with richness, depth, subtlety, highs, lows, kindness, pain, grief, joy, and wonder. Just as life is always.

We hope that you can find meaning in this experience and detach from collective beliefs about what this means to you and to others. Your understanding of your journey is important. And it is yours alone.

———————— Invocation ————————

Angels, please help me detach from making meaning of my experience, so that I can find peace and acceptance right now.

Guiding Angels:
Archangel Chamuel, Archangel Faith, Archangel Michael

DAY 92

Channelled Angel message

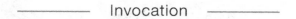

We will never judge you. We accept and love you, always.

We see that many of you have a belief that there is a judgement day after death.

We want to correct this and say unequivocally that there is no judgement day. Now or ever.

There is only ever love.

There is only ever forgiveness.

There is only ever compassion.

There is only ever unconditional acceptance.

We see you, we understand every aspect of who you are and what has led you here to now.

We wish to assist you to let go of fear and specifically the fear of judgement day.

This belief has kept a separation and distance between humans and the divine for too long.

Our love is eternal and endless. Nothing will ever stop us loving and supporting you.

When you return to the light, you are welcomed, loved, healed, and accepted wholly.

Everyone. For everything. We understand that this notion can be confusing for many of you, however, it is truth.

Right now, today, we wish you to open to the message that there is nothing to fear in working with us. There is nothing we see within you that we do not fully accept and love.

You are magnificent and loveable exactly as you are.

Invocation

Angels, please help me let go of all walls, fears and beliefs that create separation between my heart and the divine. Please let me practise self-acceptance and open to unconditional acceptance from the divine.

Guiding Angels:
Archangel Zadkiel, Archangel Azrael, Archangel Chamuel

DAY 93

Channelled Angel message

There is a collective and individual experience now.

Everything is connected.

There have always been overlapping themes between the individual and collective, but this is more visible now.

As the vibration on Earth shifts, and more light floods Earth, there is mass disruption and dismantling of veils and illusions.

Truth is being revealed. For the individual and the collective.

Clarity and truth are coming in waves.

Individual awareness and understanding shifts the collective awareness and understanding.

What you are experiencing now was destined and you chose to be here now.

This time is miraculous. Change, creation, death, transition, birth, rebirth all are occuring now.

We invite you to remember that you are supported by the divine now.

We invite you to notice the themes that are presenting for you and around you now.

We invite you to detach from the collective consciousness and be discerning and curious about the experience unfolding.

We invite you to slow down and allow space around you now, in order to move through your own awakening.

Invocation

Angels, please help me become aware of the collective consciousness, and let go of any beliefs that no longer support my highest good.

Guiding Angels: Archangel Haniel, Archangel Nathaniel

DAY 94

Channelled Angel message

When you work with us, light fills your whole being.

It doesn't take long for you to learn how to feel our energy and receive the light.

The light is available to every human.

The light is love.

There are many factors that disconnect you from the light now, and we wish to help you reclaim access to it.

Working with us has no requirements.

We are not religious, and we do not require you to be.

We can and will work with every human who asks and will be with you the instant that you call on us.

As you begin to trust and open to our energy, you will feel washed with love, as if you are flooded with light.

For some, this will be the first time in a long time that you have experienced unconditional love, and this might cause an emotional response of intense joy or even grief as you remember your birthright to access this divine love of source.

This intensity will settle. This love is not a scary or bad thing.

Light and love are available to you always.

Working with us can help you open your heart and energy to remember this and access it.

When you first begin, you will find it easiest to connect to us in nature, or in meditation.

With practice, you will be able to feel our light, love and guidance anywhere.

Angels, please help me open to the feeling of unconditional love, so that I might also love myself and others unconditionally.

Guiding Angels: Archangel Chamuel, Archangel Zadkiel

DAY 95

Channelled Angel message

We invite you to create boundaries now.

We invite you to create physical and energetic space around you.

We invite you to detach from the collective, from the hive of sleeping.

We invite you to notice where you have been enmeshed with people, structures or beliefs that no longer serve you.

We invite you to step back both literally and energetically.

We invite you to create room for you to grow into the space that is created during this process.

We invite you to grow into yourself. To become aware of your own journey. Your own beliefs. Your own truths.

Much will be revealed now. This is subjective and the only truths that matter are the ones that matter to you.

With space and distance, you will see things with a new perspective. Yours.

———— Invocation ————

Angels, please help me follow my own path and create boundaries where needed so that I can discover my true self.

Guiding Angels: Archangel Michael, Archangel Nathaniel

DAY 96

Channelled Angel message

Everyone can learn to speak with us.

We are coming through now because you are ready.

We are bringing new messages now because the awakening is occurring.

We are coming through now to remind you that you can work with us directly, and that this can make life easier during challenging times.

We are coming through now because we see a transformation occurring and your own experience of transformation is part of this.

We are coming through now because you are ready to work with us.

We want you to know that we are not religious, we hold no judgement ever, and we are always loving and compassionate. Always.

We want you to know that we will never give you messages that make you feel afraid.

We want you to know that we would never laugh at you, shame you, belittle you, be angry with you, or tell you that you have made a mistake. This is how you discern our messages from those who do not serve unconditional love.

We will always show you the next step to the best possible outcome and will always respect your free will to choose another path.

We want you to know that working with us feels like love. Always.

We want you to know that it is not as hard as you think to learn to speak with us.

Angels, please help me be discerning as I open to work with you.
Please be clear and strong with your guidance so that I learn to
discern your tone and energy of unconditional love.

Guiding Angels:
Archangel Uriel, Archangel Raziel, Archangel Michael

DAY 97

Channelled Angel message

Look inwards to find your way through this experience.

The answers you seek are available to you within.

You are far stronger and far more resilient than you realise.

You can and will find your way through this experience.

Silence and quiet are needed now.

Your inner voice speaks softly and with love. How can you make space around you to hear it?

Go to nature. Clear the noise. Switch off from all distractions.

There is a strong feeling of truth within you that will speak clearly if you give it space.

You have always been your most powerful teacher. All we do is offer suggestions, love, support, validation.

It is more important for you to speak up now than ever.

But first, take time to find yourself in the quiet.

This might feel uncomfortable at first if you are not used to silence.

Your inner voice will show itself to you with feelings, ideas, inspiration, and tears.

Angels, please help me create space and quiet so that I can hear my needs, feelings, ideas, and truth now.

Guiding Angels: Archangel Nathaniel

DAY 98

Channelled Angel message

We want you to know that even when things feel dark, there are miracles.

We know that sometimes there are experiences that are so challenging, so painful, that it is hard to understand or find meaning.

The reasons for suffering may seem hard to understand.

Pain and suffering are a part of the human experience. It has always been so.

We ask you to practise acceptance over that which you cannot change and let go.

We ask you to look for the love in the situation, for it is always there. This is where you begin to find the miracles.

This is where you begin to find hope.

Love is always the answer. It is the pathway through the experience. It is how you can make sense of pain and suffering, and it is the gateway to faith.

Love is the energy that reminds you of your oneness.

Love is an energy of the creation force, and allowing yourself to feel love, even during pain and suffering, will change your experience of life and open you to miracles.

Miracles always exist, but sometimes we cannot see them until we are ready.

Joy is in every experience, even in death. Joy exists in even the most painful circumstances. Both joy and love can be found even on the darkest days.

Today we simply ask you to acknowledge this message, and we send our love flowing through to your heart, so that you can honour both the darkness and the light around you, or in your experience right now.

For both exist, and neither is better or worse. They both are just a part of your experience.

<hr />

Invocation

Angels, please assist me when all I can see is darkness, pain, and grief. Please remind me that there is also love, joy and miracles.

Guiding Angels:
Archangel Chamuel, Archangel Azrael, Archangel Jophiel

DAY 99

Channelled Angel message

We want you to know that life is meant to include experiences of both light and shadow.

We want you to know that there is beauty, joy, and love in all your experiences, even the painful ones.

We remind you that when you face adversity and challenges, these are still experiences of learning about love.

You are filled with love. It never ends. Your resilience, creativity and faith amazes us, and fills us with joy and awe.

We want you to know that it's ok to find some experiences challenging.

We want you to breathe out and find some peace within,

knowing that the lighter times will return.

We want you to soften into faith and let that love within you lead you forwards when things feel difficult.

There is light all around you now. There is love all around you now. And always.

You are radiant and filled with light and love!

When you find it hard to feel this love, we ask you to go to nature. We will find you there.

<hr/>

Invocation

Angels, please remind me that I can access infinite love in nature. I give you permission to interrupt my day when I most need it with a reminder to go to nature.

Guiding Angels: Guardian Angels

DAY 100

Channelled Angel message

We want you to know that there is magic around you now.

We want you to know that as the vibration of Earth changes, and more light floods the earth, you will find the distance between an idea and it manifesting into reality becomes smaller. Even instant.

Sometimes you call this magic. It is the creation force. It is energy. It is love in motion.

We also want you to know that your own ability to harness this creative energy has never been more potent, more powerful, or more important than now.

We want you to remember that creativity is joy! And that your imagination is an extension of your connection to the divine.

What you can imagine can become real.

Have you seen this already? Have you noticed how, when you open yourself to the divine, to faith, when you are unattached and open, miraculous occurrences happen out of the blue?

We want you to know that even though there are challenging times, the light has never been more present. That joy, wonder and magic is swirling all around you now.

If you are finding it hard to access this feeling now, we remind you:

- Go to nature. Place your body on the earth or in the ocean.
- Listen to music that you love.
- Immerse yourself in creative expressions that you love, or
- Anything that helps you laugh and raise your vibration.

You are filled with love! This is what makes you human. It is what makes you feel everything so deeply. It is your very special gift.

There is magic manifesting now.

———— Invocation ————

Angels, please help me access my inspiration and express my ideas, dreams, and feelings. Please help me create what I dream now.

Guiding Angels:
Archangel Ariel, Archangel Chamuel, Archangel Sandalphon

DAY 101

Channelled Angel message

We want you to know that you're not alone.

We want you to notice all the love in your life right now. Look around you at the people who are making their love felt to you now.

We want you to know that we love you, and we are here with you now and always.

We want you to know that the animals, birds, and fish will be showing themselves to you every day to sing *We are with you, we love you, we are one.*

We want you to know that the faeries and all the elementals are whispering and awakening to make their love felt to you now.

We want you to know that your ancestors are sending their love, their support, and their wisdom through your genetic tree now.

We want you to know that your Guardian Angels are surrounding you with their protection, love and strength now.

We want you to know that the gods, goddesses and ascended masters are flooding their love and support to you now.

We want you to open yourself to this love, this support, and let it radiate through you now.

We want you to know that Gaia, Mother Earth, is with you now and ALWAYS, and her energy is flowing through you like a wonderful current of light now.

You are not alone.

You are connected to all living things, and you are loved.

——————— Invocation ———————

Angels, please help me open to receive love in my life, from you and from all beings who are aligned with unconditional love.

Guiding Angels:
Archangel Chamuel, Archangel Ariel, Archangel Uriel

DAY 102

Channelled Angel message

Everything is changing now. You will be ok.

There is a significant experience occurring now.

There is light flooding the earth. Everything is being illuminated now.

This is creating intense internal reactions of both shock and joy. Everything feels heightened. This is because the vibration is changing as light floods the earth, allowing you to feel and see more.

You will now begin to see everything differently.

This experience is happening on both an individual and collective level. Both are connected. You are connected to everything.

Your awareness and perception will shift and change rapidly now. And it will seem as if everything is changing around you. And it is.

Your way forwards through this change is via love.

Your personal responsibility is to be yourself!

This is a loving action and all you need to do. If you focus on being yourself, everything will flow as it needs to, at the exact right pace. Every other action and decision you need to make will come more easily if you allow yourself to be completely 'you'.

The rapidity of the change you are experiencing will feel uncomfortable at times.

Your identity will come under the spotlight. Your sense of community will come under the spotlight. Your values will come under the spotlight.

Just be you.

You will be ok.

This is a wonderful time for you and the collective, a time of miraculous change and great awakening.

Angels, please help me navigate this time of change by softening into my fully expressed authentic self.

Guiding Angels:
Archangel Nathaniel, Archangel Faith, Archangel Grace

DAY 103

Channelled Angel message

This time is here to show you everything that matters to you.

We invite you to open your heart now and be curious.

What is being shown to you now? What is being revealed?

What makes you feel passionate, angry, sad, joyful, inspired, happy or loving?

There is a wonderful experience unfolding for you and for all humanity.

Possibility and miracles are an energy you can reach out and grasp like never before.

For some, this process of distillation, or purification, might feel like a rebirth. Like a phoenix rising from the ashes.

This might feel uncomfortable or exciting, depending on the day. This is a powerful process that the collective is experiencing together and individually.

We invite you to be curious, playful, and expressive.

If grief, anger, or rage come up, we invite you to notice what path this leads you on. This is important. What needs to be expressed more through you now?

If you feel joyful, grateful, elated, excited, we invite you to express this now, and see where it takes you. This is your heart guiding you to grow into your full potential now.

There is no right or wrong way to process this experience. Only your way. Sovereign self-expression is key. What do you love? What do you feel passion for? What do you feel dislike or anger for, to the degree that you feel you must speak up and act?

This process is not as it seems.

It is much better.

─────────── Invocation ───────────

Angels, please show me what I cannot see, so that I can express my fully realised authentic self.

Guiding Angels:
Archangel Haniel, Archangel Nathaniel, Archangel Faith

DAY 104

Channelled Angel message

As you become aware of new realities now, know that you are filled with light.

There is a collective experience of truths being revealed now.

You will see this on an individual and collective level.

At times, it might seem as if great darkness is coming to light.

There is also great love being awakened and expressed.

This journey will bring light to both, as both are part of the human experience.

As you navigate your own experience of changing awareness, we want you to know that even though this may be difficult and painful at times, you are not alone.

We want to speak about the human spirit.

Humans are amazing. You are filled with the same force that creates stars, flowers, sunshine, and rainbows. You are walking, living, and breathing miracles. Love is the core of your being. You are light, you are love.

At times, you might feel disconnected from this truth, from your source.

We want to remind you that you are in fact one with the creation force, with God as you understand that concept, with the universe, with all living beings, with SOURCE.

You are filled with light. You are filled with love!

You are wonderful, creative, imperfect, emotional, capable, resilient, imaginative, caring, AMAZING beings.

We want you to remember that you are light and love now. That light and love are the pathway through all darkness.

———————— Invocation ————————

Angels, please help me see light in the darkness, and feel peace with the change and revelations occurring in my life and in the world.

Guiding Angels:
Archangel Chamuel, Archangel Faith, Archangel Michael

DAY 105

Channelled Angel message

It is important to speak your truth now, and we will support you.

We know that you have already felt or seen this message in your life.

We want to confirm the guidance you have received.

As you navigate your current experience, you may have noticed that you feel more passionate than previously.

You might also be noticing that you feel clearer and have a

stronger sense of what is important to you.

Many of you will also be experiencing what feels like an activation. A call to service. A call to action. A call to step up, step into your light path (however that looks for you) and speak up and share the vision of a new way.

There is no right or wrong here; it is your truth from your heart.

There is no longer a need to hide in the shadows. In fact, it is more important than ever to fully express all parts of yourself without shame.

Love will guide you now.

Your opinion, ideas, voice, work, teachings, art, actions, and example are needed urgently.

Whatever steps you have been guided to take, we wish to confirm: yes, this is the time!

Your voice and vision are needed now.

We will support and guide you.

You have so much love and support around you now. Just ask, and we will make our presence felt to you in signs, music, nature, and messages.

———————— Invocation ————————

Angels, please help me speak up and share my truth as I see it and feel it in my heart now.

Guiding Angels:
Archangel Nathaniel, Archangel Michael, Archangel Gabriel

DAY 106

Channelled Angel message

This is a time of fire, death, and rebirth.

We want you to know that these cycles are always present.

We want you to know that great change sometimes comes quickly, with fire and death.

We want you to know that we mean spiritual death, however, this sometimes also coincides with physical death.

We want you to know that acceptance is the pathway through this experience, for it has always been so with human life.

We want you to know that this is an unusual time in that there is a collective experience in the cycle unfolding now.

We want you to know that a cycle such as this will have moments of intensity and also moments of bliss.

We want you to know that there is immense support around you—you the individual—and around the collective: loving support from light beings, as well as actual human support. Many are working in the light. Including you. We see your work, dear one.

Open your heart now to the truths being revealed within. Your own truths are the gateway through your own spiritual journey through the fire, through the metaphorical death and into your own rebirth.

Remember, dear one, you chose to be here now, and you are light.

———————— Invocation ————————

Angels, please assist me to shed any remaining walls or veils so that I can see my pathway clearly and be reborn now.

Guiding Angels:
Archangel Nathaniel, Archangel Zadkiel, Archangel Chamuel

DAY 107

Channelled Angel message

We want you to forget everything you think you know about Angels.

We want you to experience our energy and our messages yourself and learn through us.

We want you to know that you can work with us regardless of whether you think you have a gift, or think you are worthy or intuitive enough.

Everyone can speak with us and learn how to hear our guidance. You have done this before. This knowledge already exists in your light body and higher consciousness, waiting to be awakened.

You are worthy because you are human.

There is no special gift. Everyone can learn to use their intuition and to speak with the divine. Some are further along the path than others, but all have this potential within them.

We remind you that Angel communication is fun, loving, compassionate and accepting.

We remind you that we do not judge you, feel anger towards you, or feel disappointment about your choices or actions. Ever.

We remind you that we love you unconditionally, always.

We remind you that every single human being has Angels who are with them every single moment of their life on Earth.

We remind you that we are not religion, we are love.

We remind you that there is nothing to fear in working with us; we will never scare you, harm you, give you messages that would frighten you, or interfere with your free will. We will also not bypass truth and will help you find acceptance with the full spectrum of the human experience, including the painful and shadow aspects.

We remind you that we are lighthearted and fun. We love music, we love creativity, we love seeing you express yourself fully, and we love supporting you in whichever way is most needed.

Our task is to support you in achieving self-actualisation through realisation.

We invite you to feel the light and love that we are sending to you now.

We invite you to trust the signs you are already receiving.

———————— Invocation ————————

Angels, please help me identify and release any stories, beliefs or blocks about my worth or ability to work with you so that I am able to connect with you on a deeper level now.

Guiding Angels:
Archangel Uriel, Archangel Faith, Archangel Michael

DAY 108

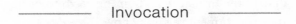
Angel lesson: Archangel Ariel

Archangel Ariel is the Angel of the natural world and manifesting.

Archangel Ariel works with all consciousness in the natural world, including plants, animals, faeries and elementals.

Her energy feels bubbly, powerful, light, uplifting, energising and empowering.

She has new messages for the current Earth experience.

She asks you to remember that you are an energetic being in circuitry with the earth and all living beings, both known and unknown.

She asks you to remember that you are abundantly provided for by the earth always.

She asks you to remember that the natural world works to support you, and that the animals are communicating with all humans now to support you through this current experience. In fact, you have a soul contract with the earth, and all plants and animals, as they experience aspects of realisation in relationship with you.

She reminds you that you are healthiest when your energy is in regular circuitry and contact with the earth, and that this energy supports you through your frequency shifts. So please allow yourself time in nature and on the earth to bring yourself into frequency alignment regularly now.

She reminds you that the collective story of abundance is different from the truth of abundance, which is your true birthright.

She reminds you that you are one with ALL living beings and that this recollection is part of your individual and collective experience now.

For all Earth and animal healers, she asks to work with you and support you to activate your purpose now.

 Invocation

Archangel Ariel, I invite you to work with me. Please help me reconnect to the earth and to find harmony with all living beings. Please help me open to the true abundance of life on Earth and recall that everything I desire is already available to me in miraculous abundance.

Guiding Angel: Archangel Ariel
Energy: Feminine
Aura colour: White, gold & pink

DAY 109

Channelled Angel message

We invite you to notice the softness and peace flooding Earth now.

We invite you to notice your own energy softening, your heart chakra opening.

We invite you to become more aware of the vibrations that Earth is emitting and sending through your own energetic circuit now (as always, but you are more attuned now).

We invite you to notice your vibrational attunement to Earth, to other living beings, to nature and to animals.

We invite you to notice how your physical body is feeling now, and how this is changing.

But mostly, we invite you to notice how your heart feels now.

Have you noticed the love flooding through you? Have you noticed that you feel more peaceful? Have you noticed that you feel more sensitive, more loving, happier, and more connected?

To experience this more, you can work with Archangel Chamuel, as well as spend more time outdoors in nature.

—————— Invocation ——————

Angels, please help me soften and open to the infinite loving energy of the divine now. Please remind me to spend time in nature to both access this energy and process this shift on a mind, body, and spirit level.

Guiding Angels:
Archangel Chamuel, Archangel Ariel, Archangel Gersisa

DAY 110

Channelled Angel message

This is an individual and collective process of great change and awakening occurring now, and you will be ok.

We are here now to assist you through this shift.

We see tremendous and wonderful change occurring.

We see all aspects of this change, and we know that for some, at times it can feel challenging, painful, and dark. We also see experiences of miracles, light, love, compassion, kindness, creativity, healing, new awareness, and realisation.

We see you speaking up.

We see you asking for what you need and setting boundaries.

We see you navigating change with resilience, hope, and love and compassion.

We see you awakening to new realities and perspectives.

We see you making changes that feel helpful, positive, and inspired.

We see so much positive, love-based, light-based action right now; we remind you to search for this too.

We acknowledge that there is a broadcast of fear being transmitted and experienced in the collective. We remind you that this has been present for a long time, and for this to shift and disperse, it must first be acknowledged.

As you navigate your awakening and begin to see the darkness and fear in the world around you, we want you to know that we can work with you in a much greater capacity than you have previously imagined possible.

We remind you that our support does not violate your free will.

We work with the light of the infinite one creator and are a conscious expression of unconditional love. You will always know us by this one aspect.

Angels, please assist me through my one awakening experience, as I become more aware of other realities and perspectives. Please help me release all fear.

Guiding Angels:
Archangel Haniel, Archangel Michael, Archangel Nathaniel

DAY 111

Channelled Angel message

We are constantly giving you signs and messages.

Our communication begins gently, with signs that you can easily recognise because they make you feel joyful instantly.

We will never give you fear-based messages, ever.

Our messages are always in your highest good and are often a redirection of your focus and attention to a pathway that you have not yet explored.

Working with us is not about seeing the future or being able to skip the process of life.

Our messages and signs always respect your free will. You can always choose a different pathway from the one we present to you. We present options, choices and pathways that already exist. The choice is always yours to make.

The future is fluid, changeable, and not set in stone.

Whilst there are certain relationships that you may have a soul contract to explore, there is still freedom within these soul contracts.

When you feel disconnected, isolated, or alone, we are right there with you, and will offer loving guidance every time you ask.

The easiest way to contact us when you first begin is in nature.

The more you raise your vibration to the frequency of love, the easier it is to hear our guidance, as fear contracts your energy field and creates filters that act as noise.

Everyone can learn to hear our messages.

Everyone is worthy of working with us.

─────── Invocation ───────

Angels, please help me raise my vibration so that I can hear, feel, and see your messages more easily. Please give me signs that I will easily recognise.

Guiding Angels:
Archangel Haniel, Archangel Metatron, Archangel Michael

DAY 112

Channelled Angel message

There is an energetic experience occurring now. The energy is changing.

The frequency of Earth has been rising rapidly. It is still rising. It is aligning to a higher frequency of light and love.

Many of you will be aware of this change and can feel strong physical sensations of energy moving through your body at peak energetic times. Some of you will become aware that you experience profound shifts in consciousness after each energetic upgrade.

Some of you are here to assist this change by anchoring the new light frequencies first.

At times, this might feel like intense work. We can assist you to receive, integrate and anchor the new light frequencies on a mind, body, and spirit level.

We remind you that you chose to be here now to participate in and assist this process.

As the frequency of Earth changes, there is both an individual and collective shift, for both are one. As the light increases, the darkness is exposed. As the light increases, more souls are attuned to the light and to love.

At times, this awakening can feel difficult, even painful, as with this process comes awareness and clarity. Realisation and revelation are a part of this process.

The most efficient way to process and integrate new light frequencies in your own mind, body and spirit is to spend time in nature.

Please allow your physical and energetic body the support it needs through this powerful energetic process.

Use your own light practice as your pathway through this shift: choose actions that bring your vibration back into harmony, into the light, and into love.

─────── Invocation ───────

Angels, please remind me to spend time in nature, and to focus on raising my vibration as my highest priority now.

Guiding Angels:
Archangel Metatron, Archangel Gersisa, Archangel Ariel

DAY 113

Channelled Angel message

There is a significant collective and individual experience occurring now. This is presenting both physically and spiritually.

This level of shift and change has not occurred since Atlantis.

This is a monumental vibrational, consciousness and physical shift.

Please allow yourself time to move through this experience and process the shift.

This is a transition time of much change.

This requires patience, discernment, time, curiosity, and faith, and most of all love.

You will be ok. Humanity will be ok.

There is more light coming to Earth than ever before.

All you need do is follow your own guidance and step further into your own awakening process now. Your participation is required. Your individual journey is a part of the collective experience.

It is time to remember your mission now.

———————— Invocation ————————

Angels, please help me remember my mission and pathway now.

Guiding Angels: Archangel Michael, Archangel Faith

DAY 114

Angel lesson: Archangel Haniel

Archangel Haniel helps with intuition, awakening, flow and the divine feminine.

She is here to support you now through your spiritual awakening.

She works with the Earth energies of flow, with the tides and moon cycles, with surrender and faith.

She can help you find peace with your feminine aspects (regardless of whether you are a man or woman) and assists all who have a soul contract to anchor the new 5D feminine expression.

She helps you release any discomfort or fear that you feel as your intuition increases.

She helps you flow with the energy around you and listen and be in sync with the energies you experience.

She invites you to let go of resistance and soften into your experience of expressing power.

She supports you to remember that emotions and the feminine are safe to express.

She asks you to bring your awareness to where you might be out of flow, out of balance, or operating solely in a masculine expression.

She invites you to bring awareness to the receiving, waiting, flowing, creating, expressing, feeling.

You will know it is time to work with her if you find these areas challenging.

She asks you to journal, draw, and sit in the discomfort of waiting and not knowing (as this is where breakthroughs, guidance, inspiration, intuition, and flow are found).

She points out that, as a collective, this experience is presenting you with the perfect opportunity to practise and heal all of these areas within yourself, and she assures you that it is not a coincidence that the collective needs to balance the feminine aspect now in order to move into the new paradigm.

Invocation

Archangel Haniel, I invite you to work with me. Please help me feel safe as I open my intuition. Please help me heal my divine feminine aspect. Please help me feel in flow with the forces of nature.

DAY 115

Channelled Angel message

The highest priority for you now is to follow your heart. Love is vital now.

We know that for some of you, this time is challenging.

We remind you that this is a transition period. An awakening.

We remind you that this is a time of deep heart expansion.

We invite you to allow yourself time to adjust to a slower pace.

We invite you to allow yourself time to adjust to new frequencies of light and love.

We invite you to notice your own energy adjusting to the new light frequencies and how this shifts your awareness and perspective.

We invite you to know that there is an attunement happening now.

We invite you to know that your heart is the way through this.

We invite you to know that you are safe to give and receive love, and you are opening to more love than you have ever experienced.

We remind you that your identity is transforming now.

You are becoming, realising, expressing, emerging.

We remind you that there is a DNA and light-body activation occurring now.

It is a love activation. A purpose activation.

We remind you that you chose to be here now to both embody and assist this frequency shift.

We remind you that you are a light carrier: you are anchoring the light now.

We remind you that every time you attune yourself more to love, you also assist the light frequencies to anchor more deeply in the collective consciousness.

──────── Invocation ────────

Angels, please help me always find the pathway of love and light as I embody my own experience of this shift in consciousness.

Guiding Angels: Archangel Chamuel, Archangel Metatron

DAY 116

Channelled Angel message

Your highest priority is to focus on the light now. On love.

We remind you that you are experiencing a great shift now.

On some days, this might feel difficult or even deeply troubling for you.

On some days, a great darkness is being presented to you, perhaps for the first time. We honour this experience. It can be a challenging and painful process to see the darkness that was hidden.

We remind you that you can get through this. That you chose to be here now. That this experience is not only dark, but also filled with magnificent light.

We remind you that the way through the darkest times, now and always, is by focusing on the light.

This is not spiritual bypassing or naivety. You will notice, understand, accept, and feel pain, and then this experience will take you somewhere.

To balance this, we ask you to look to the light and remember that you are a deeply loving being filled with light.

We ask you to remember and awaken to the truth that exists within.

You are not separate or alone; you are connected to the divine and to all living beings.

We remind you to immerse yourself in the light and the love that already exists in your life.

And when you are ready, we also ask you to work with us, for you are also a light bringer.

———————— Invocation ————————

Angels, please help me see the full spectrum of my current experience, so that I do not lose hope. Please show me the light now.

Guiding Angels:
Archangel Butyalil, Archangel Michael, Archangel Nathaniel

DAY 117

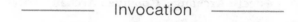

We remind you that when you speak your truth, your light shines brighter.

We remind you that there is a great need for you to shine your light now.

We remind you that the way through the dark times is via shining your own light as brightly as you can.

This is as simple as it sounds.

Just be you.

Express all parts of yourself.

When you see a truth, a boundary, a line, speak it.

When you feel deeply passionate about something, allow that to be expressed.

When you feel overwhelmed with joy or love, let it shine and flow and grow!

What do you love? Who do you love?

What do you now see that you cannot do, be, or tolerate anymore?

How can you find a clearer, stronger, more truthful version of your soul expression now?

How is your current experience gifting you with clarity now?

What personal truth has been revealed to you?

How can you action this?

There is always a way forward. We can assist you. Take it slowly. Step by step. Remember: this is a time of transition and change.

Every time you speak your truth now, you create more light within your own energy field, and this becomes a beacon to those around you. You become a light bringer.

So, we ask you to give yourself permission to surrender to the inward journey of letting go and becoming you now.

We will support you.

—————— Invocation ——————

Angels, please help me feel safe to express all parts of myself now.

Guiding Angels:
Archangel Nathaniel, Archangel Zadkiel, Archangel Michael

DAY 118

Channelled Angel message

We want you to know that your third eye is opening now.

There is nothing about this process that you need to fear.

Any fear you feel will move through you and then pass.

There is nothing about this process that is unsafe for you.

This is happening to all humans now.

This is both a physical and energetic upgrade. You are an energetic being; your chakras are connected to source energy and to Earth energy while you are incarnate.

You are attuning to the new 5D frequencies now.

There has been a significant frequency shift that is presenting as a shift in awareness.

You may be seeing things differently, experiencing clarity, experiencing a sense of seeing truth in situations for the first time; you may be having perspective or awareness shifts.

Allow yourself time to integrate this new awareness and vision.

Everything around you is the same, and yet it is also completely different.

You are supported by us through this shift in awareness, this shift in consciousness, this awakening.

You are safe and you will adjust to this new ability to see.

It will assist you to take things slowly, and spending time in nature will assist you to acclimatise and attune to the new frequency and the higher perspective and clarity this is giving you.

--------- Invocation ---------

Angels, please assist me to see things with a new perspective on all levels now.

Guiding Angels: Archangel Haniel, Archangel Metatron

DAY 119

Channelled Angel message

There is a great change occurring now.

The change you are experiencing is happening internally and externally.

You will experience individual shifts as well as collective shifts.

At times, you might feel uneasy, unsettled, unsure, even ungrounded.

Your sense of identity is rapidly changing and transforming now.

You are becoming a purer version of yourself.

Veils are lifting now.

What you are able to now see has always been present. You are able to see it more clearly now.

We remind you to go slowly through this shift.

We remind you to spend time in nature, with your body on the earth, to help your own vibration attune to the earth vibration.

This is your highest priority to process and adjust to this change.

This is a time for a slow pace.

This is a time for softness and calm.

This is a time for reflection.

All the answers that you seek are found within.

We can assist you.

Invocation

Angels, please help me slow down and create time and space to adjust to the changes I am experiencing.

Guiding Angels: Archangel Nathaniel, Archangel Metatron

DAY 120

Channelled Angel message

When you create space and time around you to slow down, everything becomes clear.

We remind you that everything is happening for a greater purpose that you cannot see (but perhaps you sense).

This process will take some time.

We remind you that you are supported by the divine like never before.

We remind you that there is a different way to live being birthed now. The new earth pathway is slowly being revealed to you now. This is what you always knew deep down to be true.

We remind you that many deceptions have been created to hide this truth from you.

We know that sometimes these are complex and dark.

We remind you that these deceptions and structures are crumbling now. Perhaps you have noticed?

During this shift, there is light all around you.

We remind you that the way through this experience and shift is via love.

We remind you that all you need to do is follow your inner guidance and seek the pathway of unconditional love.

―――――― Invocation ――――――

Please assist me to slow down and move through my personal shifts, awakenings, and changes now.

Guiding Angels: Archangel Metatron, Archangel Haniel

DAY 121

Channelled Angel message

There is more light flooding the earth than ever before.

You can feel the light flooding in and activating you now.

You can feel your heart chakra expanding, and love flooding through you.

You can see clearly now. This is both painful and blissful.

You are moving quickly. Things are accelerating as the light anchors.

The light is dismantling and disintegrating old structures of darkness and deception. This is both deeply painful and joyous. This is both within and without.

All you need do is allow the light to guide you now.

———————— Invocation ————————

Angels, please remind me that this process is safe, and that I will be ok as I change, awaken, and see clearly now.

Guiding Angels:
Archangel Faith, Archangel Michael, Archangel Haniel

DAY 122

Channelled Angel message

We say again, Angels are not religious. Angels are light, and love, and God.

We will continue to share this message to slowly break through the collective belief otherwise.

Religion is human.

Angels are not bound by the rules of religion.

Angels abide by the spiritual laws of free will, of love, of compassion, of forgiveness, of acceptance.

We are light beings.

We are unconditional love.

We are here to serve humanity.

We work with any who ask.

We will never do harm. We will never violate your free will or that of another.

We will only guide you in ways that align with your highest good and that do not interfere with your soul contracts, your learning or your choice.

We do not foretell the future.

Our guidance is specific but shows you only possibilities so that you then have freedom to choose your own pathway.

We are always with you.

There is no time or space; we hear your prayers and questions instantly. We are never busy. We will work with ALL who ask in the moment they ask.

We will always guide you in a way that you can understand.

We will never shame you, be angry at you, be disappointed in you, speak down to you, ridicule you, laugh at you or abandon you.

There are many distorted channels, and many distorted messages. You will know a true Angelic message because it will always feel like love. It will not scare you, ask you to do something or enmesh with you. Distorted Angelic channels do not respect your sovereign free will.

When you work with us, you will feel loved, safe, and accepted unconditionally.

You will feel love and light flood your aura, and your heart will respond with sensations of love.

Everyone can learn (or remember) how to speak with us.

It is time to remember and awaken to the loving guidance of the divine now.

Invocation

Angels, please help me tune in to the clear and true Angelic frequency and reject all fear-based distortions now.

Guiding Angels:
Archangel Michael, Archangel Uriel, Archangel Raziel

DAY 123

Channelled Angel message

We want you to know that your heart is opening to the frequency of love now.

We want you to know that there is a major frequency shift occurring on Earth now.

We want you to know that the light of source, of the creator, of God—which is also the frequency of love—is flooding Earth now.

We want you to know that many human light activators are anchoring this frequency to the earth now. They are anchoring it through their physical bodies now, so that it can then grow exponentially to those around them.

You might be feeling this frequency shift now. It feels like positive, gentle loving energy flowing through your chakras.

You will feel it in your heart.

You will feel joy, lightness, sensitivity, love and all the emotions on the human spectrum.

It is calm, gentle, and peaceful. This is a love/light frequency and DNA activation.

At times, you might feel lighter.

At times, you might feel tired.

To help your physical body attune to these new frequencies, please spend time in nature with your body on the earth.

Love is activating within you and on Earth at a magnificent rate.

Light is flooding through you now.

Open to receive now.

────────── Invocation ──────────

Angels, please remind me that this experience is safe, and remind me to allow myself time in nature to integrate these new frequencies.

Guiding Angels:
Archangel Metatron, Archangel Haniel, Archangel Chamuel

DAY 124

Channelled Angel message

As you witness darkness, we ask you to be the light. Embody love/light now.

Sometimes it may seem as if all you can see is unbearable darkness.

However, we want to assure you that the light, that our light, and our love, is always with you, and closer than ever.

We want to assure you that you can shift and reconnect with this light, and our love, quickly and easily.

There are many ways you can do this.

The most powerful way is to be in nature with your body on the earth, or in the ocean.

Light meditation is also very powerful. Imagine the white

light of source flooding through each of your energy centres and clearing and opening them.

Working with us daily will raise your vibration very quickly and support you to stay connected to the light more easily.

Be loving and compassionate with your words in the face of fear, pain, and anger now.

Be loving and compassionate to yourself in your thoughts and actions now.

Remember to respond as your own heart would, even in the face of great darkness, pain or anger around you, or towards you.

The light and love of the divine can disintegrate and dismantle fear and dark energies instantly.

Every earthly challenge can be navigated with love as your guide.

Love is soft, gentle, compassionate, and kind. It is patient and slow.

Love is powerful, forgiving and accepting.

Love is a great motivator for creating action and change.

Love is flooding Earth now. Light is flooding Earth now.

Remember, you do not always need to understand your experience or what you are witnessing now. Your purpose is only to be present to the experience.

Seek the light within and radiate that light for all those around you to be uplifted by your vibration.

———————— Invocation ————————

Angels, please help me always find light/love within
and radiate love/light without.

Guardian Angels:
Archangel Chamuel, Archangel Metatron, Archangel Jophiel

DAY 125

Channelled Angel message

You are awakening now.

This is a process that is both blissful and painful.

At the core, this is a reconnection to the divine. To love.

You are safe and supported, and you will be ok.

This is remembering your true being, your sovereignty, your purpose, your light.

All humans are experiencing this to varying degrees now. Some have already done much of the work. Others are beginning now. All are experiencing a shift in frequency. All are awakening to a new level of consciousness.

The way through this is inwards, via your heart.

This is a journey of love and as such will at times include grief, anger, joy, tenderness, compassion, forgiveness and all the other aspects of love.

We remind you to be loving to yourself and others now.

We remind you to remember your connection to source, to God, and to universal consciousness now.

We remind you to anchor the light and express the love that is activating through you now.

This was always who you were. You can just see it more clearly now.

——————— Invocation ———————

Angels, please remind me that I am awakening now, and that this process is safe and filled with love.

Guiding Angels:
Archangel Haniel, Archangel Michael, Archangel Chamuel

DAY 126

Channelled Angel message

There are miraculous changes occurring now.

Whatever you previously believed possible is now limitless.

Everything that seems fixed and unchangeable is now in a state of flux and creation.

Earth has entered a new experience of reality.

The future timelines are now activating, with an outcome of light and bliss for all anchoring now.

This energy and consciousness is spreading and opening faster than you can imagine.

Your role in this outcome is still vital; your light and your love are a part of the creation process.

Continue the work you are doing to heal and to raise your frequency and consciousness now. This is your highest priority and the most important way you can serve the collective.

Miracles are beginning to form now.

Whatever your heart can imagine as possible, but improbable, is truly beginning to take shape now.

The more you anchor the light and open your heart, and embody love, the more this expands exponentially. Your actions have a far greater impact than you realise now.

─────────── Invocation ───────────

Angels, please remind me to focus on my own frequency, healing, and expansion of consciousness as my highest priority.

Guiding Angels: Archangel Metatron, Archangel Michael

DAY 127

Channelled Angel message

The most important thing you can do now is be in nature.

This will assist you with everything that is currently challenging for you.

The earth is a conscious being and able to heal you in ways you cannot imagine.

When you bring your body into full connection with the earth, you heal.

Your frequency aligns with the Earth frequency.

You release toxins.

Your heart rate drops.

Your heart opens.

You remember your 'I am' consciousness.

You remember you are not separate from Earth or other living beings.

And you feel love.

Whatever you are facing right now that is causing you pain, suffering, hurt, discomfort, or disease, we ask you to go to nature to begin to heal.

——————— Invocation ———————

Angels, please remind me of the infinite healing power of nature, and to create time to receive this unconditionally.

Guiding Angels:
Archangel Gersisa, Archangel Ariel, Archangel Raphael

DAY 128

Channelled Angel message

You are a glorious being! You are radiant, sovereign, loving and powerful!

You are remembering your worth, your power and your truth now.

You are filled with light and love that is the source of all creation.

You are capable of miracles. You create them with your thoughts and with your actions.

You are able to heal yourself and others.

You are able to do things that you cannot conceive of just now. This is emerging within you, like a remembering.

We invite you to remember that your gifts are the things you love.

We invite you to remember that your power is in loving expression of all that makes you unique.

We invite you to remember that you are unique, and your difference is your gift.

We invite you to grow the light within your heart now, and let it fill your whole being.

We remind you to share your light now. We remind you to share it as brightly as you are able to, and we will assist you with this so that you become comfortable shining brightly, for your world has conditioned you to dim your light.

We remind you to embrace your sensitive heart now, as this is your power; it is your love fully expressed and creates healthy energy flow.

Recall the truth of your radiant magnificence now.

Angels, please remind me that I am safe to express all aspects of my radiant light now.

Guiding Angels:
Archangel Jophiel, Archangel Metatron, Archangel Nathaniel

DAY 129

Channelled Angel message

As the vibrations shift, allow yourself time to adjust.

Many of you will have noticed that your life seems to have changed dramatically in a short period of time.

As the frequency of Earth rises, so does yours.

You will sometimes notice that you feel more sensitive, that you feel alternately tired or energised, that you feel joyful, then sad.

You are attuning. This can take time. But your body knows what to do, and your soul remembers the energy and vibration of love.

Any fear you feel will settle as you allow yourself time to process this shift.

Spend time in nature.

Drink pure water.

Rest as you need it.

Give yourself space to notice and understand the changes that you are experiencing.

Notice that slowing down is going to assist you through this acceleration.

Notice that you are manifesting and creating instantly now.

Notice that your previous understanding of your abilities, and your previous beliefs about yourself and the world, are all fluid and changing now.

Allow us to support you.

────── Invocation ──────

Angels, please remind me that I need space and time to adjust to the changes occurring now.

Guiding Angels: Archangel Metatron, Archangel Nathaniel

DAY 130

Channelled Angel message

In your heart, you have a memory of a different way. A different you.

For a long time, this part of you has whispered guidance.

Sometimes it feels painful when you connect here. Because everything is not as it should be. As you know it can be.

And yet, lately when you connect to this part of your heart, to this part of your soul, you have felt it awakening.

Perhaps you have had stronger feelings of love lately?

Perhaps you have felt more connected to nature, to loved ones, to us?

Perhaps your heart has been guiding you more strongly than you remember?

Perhaps at times you have felt intense grief, sadness, pain?

All of these feelings and experiences are normal now.

Your heart chakra is responding to the higher frequencies of love and light that are anchoring on Earth, and in you.

You are also responding, as you are an energetic being of light and love. You are fuelled by light and by love.

There is a reconnection to the source of all creation occurring within your energy system now; this is occurring for all humans.

Your heart chakra is awakening to the memory of its true nature. You are awakening to your memory of your true nature.

You are a gentle, loving, compassionate, miraculously creative being of love and light.

Your potential is limitless.

You chose to be here now to participate in this event.

Your role is to follow your heart.

You are love. Let love be fully expressed through you now.

—————— Invocation ——————

Angels, please assist me through my heart awakening so that I feel safe processing heightened experiences of connection and love.

Guiding Angels:
Archangel Chamuel, Archangel Raphael, Archangel Metatron

DAY 131

Channelled Angel message

There is a brand-new world emerging now.

The rate of change is rapid.

The light frequency of Earth is swiftly rising.

Your awareness and comprehension of self is changing faster than you ever recall.

You are experiencing a birth. The Earth experience is about to change. Is already changing.

You do not see it yet. You are not meant to. You see glimpses as the veil thins. You feel glimpses of lightness, of love, of change and of hope.

And then you revert back to the old way, the old density.

This is the adjustment period.

If it happened instantly, it would be too much of a shock. The amount of light would be too much for many. It would create chaos.

There is light coming in waves. As the waves come, the frequency rises.

As the frequency rises, your energy adjusts and your awareness shifts.

To adjust to this new frequency, we advise time in nature, organic foods, and pure water.

You will know what you need to do. And if you feel unsure, we remind you that the clarity will come.

There are many beings of light helping this process, both on Earth and from other places and dimensions.

There is a process underway that requires experience and embodiment.

Our guidance and love will assist you.

Let your own light radiate now as you anchor into the new love frequencies.

Trust that there is a process underway that is filled with the loving guidance of pure source energy.

─────── Invocation ───────

Angels, please remind me to stay focused on love in the moment, and to trust in the perfect divine timing of my experience.

Guiding Angels:
Archangel Nathaniel, Archangel Chamuel, Archangel Faith

DAY 132

Channelled Angel message

There are many light bringers awakening to their purpose now. You are one of them.

There is a mass awakening occurring now.

The light bringers are the catalysts in their community. The light bringers are the wayshowers to those around them.

The light bringers lead the way by anchoring the new light frequencies, by seeing visions of the new world, by processing their own awakening, by receiving the light and then shining the path for others.

Being a light bringer might feel challenging at times. For some of you, it might feel like you are alone in a world that does not understand you. This alternate vision and perspective is your gift and your purpose.

We remind you that you are not alone. You have never been alone. You have chosen to walk a path that is very important. And we are with you every step of the way.

You are being called to service now.

Every day, you are receiving new guidance and being asked to shine more brightly than ever before. It can feel vulnerable stepping into the light. And yet, you will, for you know in your heart that this is your chosen path.

The discomfort you feel at times will always pass and settle.

As you speak up, shine brightly and step into service, your confidence will grow. You will adjust and acclimatise to your new energy and radiance.

If you need guidance, ask us. We will speak to you clearly and directly so that you do not mistake the message.

There are many like you. Seek them out.

Know that this pathway is one that is supported by infinite

beings who work in the light, both on Earth and in other dimensions.

Know that your feelings are true and your sense of purpose is real.

You are on the right path, and you are not alone.

─────── Invocation ───────

Angels, please help me remember that I am not alone as I walk a pathway no one else can see. Please help me seek out and find my soul family so that I have loving friends around me on this journey.

Guiding Angels: Archangel Chamuel, Archangel Michael

DAY 133

Channelled Angel message

You are experiencing an accelerated time of personal transformation. Go slowly now.

This is a significant experience not just of your generation, but also for humanity.

This is a great awakening.

Earth is shifting. The collective is shifting. You are shifting.

Much is being revealed now. To you, and to the world.

You are experiencing rapid changes now.

This is a transition period.

There has never been a time of such rapid and significant change on Earth.

This will continue for some time and then there will be a great shift.

The change period will continue but will happen in a different way after the shift.

The shift is significant.

Until then, it will feel uncomfortable for you at times.

This intensity is necessary.

The outcome is the change that you desire.

The awareness and clarity you seek is coming.

You can make this process easier by communicating with us, by raising your vibration, by spending time in nature, and by expressing your full loving self.

Your heart knows the way forward now. This is not a thinking journey; it is a feeling journey.

Love will guide you towards the answers you seek.

Let go of attachment to when and how shifts occur. Things are not as they seem.

Invocation

Angels, please help me focus on my highest priority so that I do not get lost in my desire for specific change.

Guiding Angels: Archangel Faith, Archangel Metatron

DAY 134

Channelled Angel message

The seeds being planted now are the beginnings of miracles. A brand-new life is forming now.

Whilst at times it might feel like you are still in the darkness, we want to assure you that new life is forming now.

New pathways are being created.

Timelines are converging and the new life that you have been manifesting is now taking seed. As is the new world.

This is occurring on multiple levels and dimensions. You will begin to see signs of this in your personal life but also in your community and globally.

This is the seeding.

The creative force is now exploding within you and around you.

A subtle but important shift has occurred, and the new future is beginning to take form.

Now is the time of creation, so allow yourself time to have space to receive your divine inspiration and the next steps on your own pathway now.

This is a potent time.

Please continue to go slowly, as the full picture is not complete; there are months, even years before the full reality is birthed. Allow yourself to experience this transition period, the in-between time. The ending and beginning time when both overlap.

Death and rebirth are occurring simultaneously.

This is truly a miraculous time.

Invocation

Angels, please help me anchor into the present moment so that I may be a channel and conduit for the new earth energies birthing now.

Guiding Angels:
Archangel Nathaniel, Archangel Metatron, Archangel Faith

DAY 135

Note from Shunanda

Please, as you read this, imagine your heart chakra opening, and let the energy of hope and love fill your heart. It feels INCREDIBLE.

Channelled Angel message

Everything is possible now. The shift has begun.

We want you to know that great change is underway.

We want you to know that whilst you will experience this on a practical level in your life and the world around you, it is far greater than just that.

The changes you are experiencing are multidimensional. They are energetic.

This is the greatest shift humanity has experienced.

Earth is attuning to a higher frequency now.

The veils of fear that have been operational for time immemorial are thinning in waves and will continue to disperse.

The hearts and minds of humanity are experiencing a mass awakening.

These are exceptional times.

You chose to be here now.

Your heart is awakening to deeper love than you remember feeling.

This will at times feel deeply joyful, at times confusing, at times painful.

Your perceptions and awareness are changing rapidly.

Your identity is shifting.

Your experience is reflecting this.

The possibilities birthing now are limitless!

Whatever you can conceive of has miraculously begun to take form the very moment you imagine it.

Allow yourself to imagine deeply and often, dear one, as your heart creates this new reality! Let your feelings explore your desires, let yourself hope, and feel the joy of your tentative new imagining! For it is the creation force that you explore now. As you feel, you create.

Your heart is the miracle force.

Your love was the secret power all along.

───────────── Invocation ─────────────

Angels, please remind me that I am safe to feel, safe to dream, and safe to imagine a better world now. Please remind me of the power of my dreams so that I may be a co-creator of the new reality.

Guiding Angels:
Archangel Chamuel, Archangel Haniel, Archangel Ariel

DAY 136

Channelled Angel message

During this shift, we invite you to look for a simpler way. Things won't feel so hard soon.

As the energy shifts, your heart experiences an opening.

As the energy shifts, all your chakras receive the love and light of source to a much higher level via light-code activations occurring for all beings now.

It is far easier to receive this light as the veil thins rapidly now. You can learn to hold yourself in open connection to this light at all times. You will gradually and over time attune to this permanent source connection. It will come in waves as you adjust to holding higher light frequencies.

As the frequency shifts, the veils lift, and you will see things differently.

We invite you to be curious now. Things will continue to change very rapidly, so allow space for you to soften and unfold into this new heart frequency. The 5D frequency is love.

What can be done in a different way that feels loving now? What can be approached with a view to finding a simpler solution?

We are closer than ever before and whispering guidance to help you see your way through this shift.

It's not so hard in the new world. In fact, it's much easier. Gentler. And more loving.

--------- Invocation ---------

Angels, please help me attune to the higher frequencies and find a new way of experiencing life that is guided by love.

Guiding Angels:
Archangel Chamuel, Archangel Faith, Archangel Nathaniel

DAY 137

Channelled Angel message

This energy you feel flooding through you is love. Light codes are love expressed as light.

We invite you to recall this feeling and know that it is love and light based.

We remind you that as you spend time in nature, you will open and attune to this new higher frequency rapidly.

This light/love frequency activates through your chakras, and you will feel it first in your heart chakra.

At times, this energy might feel uncomfortable. There is nothing to fear. You will adjust quickly to this frequency.

This light frequency is healing you now. This light frequency has the power to create all the healing you desire. This light frequency is creation force expressed. It is you.

We want you to know that this light frequency has now reached a point where it will be perceptible to a large percentage of you.

This process is accelerating for all beings now. As you receive and anchor this new light frequency, you will also assist the collective acceleration.

All living beings are experiencing this shift now.

If you are a light bringer, your role is important now. Embrace the light flooding through you now. Radiate this light for all those you interact with now. This is a compassionate and non-judgemental process, dear light bringer. All you need to do is anchor the light through your heart.

Know that the animals and Gaia thank you for your service to light and to universal consciousness now.

This is the new Earth frequency. All is possible here. All is love here.

——————— Invocation ———————

Angels, I open to be a receiver of the new high-frequency light codes now, and to anchor and radiate this light for all humanity.

Guiding Angels: Archangel Butyalil, Archangel Metatron

DAY 138

Channelled Angel message

This time is the emergence. Change occurs in small steps, slowly. The new way is different to before.

As you adjust and change and grow, we remind you that there

is a divine order and timing to your process, and to the greater process.

Your process of ascension is connected to the Earth ascension.

You are a finely tuned energetic being of love. You do not need to push or rush or control this process. Everything is exactly as it should be, and everything is flowing to you in perfect order.

Your heart and mind are shifting as the frequencies shift.

You will flow and expand with this process, and then you will notice your old ways again. The veiled fearful ways. The whispers of *faster, hurry, not enough, take action, control this.*

Be gentle with yourself as you move through this transition time. The emergence is a beautiful time, and at times also awkward and uncomfortable.

Perfection can be gently put to the side now. We remind you that slow is sometimes faster.

When you surrender to the divine order of the greater process, you step out of the way and let miracles flow to you.

So, go slowly now. Gently. Softly. With love for yourself and those around you.

Honour the emergence. This is a sacred birth time.

—————— Invocation ——————

Angels, please remind me to let go and be one with the birth process occurring in my experience now.

Guiding Angels: Archangel Nathaniel

DAY 139

Channelled Angel message

Trust the process occurring now. Trust yourself.

This awakening is a journey.

Time is both speeding up and slowing down now.

You are integrating waves of frequency shifts.

You are still changing, understanding, expanding, growing, and processing.

This is a significant experience. It is nowhere near complete.

We ask you to lean on us now and surrender to divine universal love. There is energetic support from us, from Mother Gaia, from all plants and animals, and from other light beings. There is a universal love source that you and all beings are connected to. We all wish to see you succeed now. Soften your precious heart and open to our loving guidance.

You are safe to trust and have faith. There is no danger in love.

Soften and trust that you are a powerful being of radiant love.

Trust and soften into the remembering of your true worth.

Trust and soften into the knowing that there is a vast loving network here to assist you.

Trust and soften into recalling our whispers and reconnecting in dialogue with us.

Awaken.

──────── Invocation ────────

Angels, please assist me to soften and open to the infinite love of the divine now.

Guiding Angels: Archangel Haniel, Archangel Chamuel

DAY 140

Channelled Angel message

During this process, you may at times feel alone or different.

You are here to usher in the new world.

There is a process of great change underway now.

Your role is important, even vital.

For those of you who have always felt too much, felt too soft, too emotional, too intuitive, too empathic, too kind, too feminine, not masculine enough, not enough: we speak to you now.

Your difference is your purpose.

Your difference is your power.

You are you for a reason, and you are needed.

We ask you; how can you be more you?

How can you choose to shine, speak, share, create, love, or lead more now?

For that is your purpose and mission now.

Softness and love, gentle compassion, firm but loving boundaries, radical self-expression, joy—all are needed now.

All you need to do is gently, slowly unfurl your tender heart now.

Blossom into radiant and full soul expression now.

Open to the light now.

Love your way into your purpose now.

We will assist you now.

───────── Invocation ─────────

Angels, please help me feel courageous and brave as I express all that was hidden and radiate all that I am now.

Guiding Angels: Archangel Nathaniel, Archangel Michael

DAY 141

Channelled Angel message

This is a significant time of rebirth and change. It's ok to ask for support now.

You are experiencing a major period of transformation now. As is Gaia, your home, the earth.

This change affects all living beings.

This change will result in unity consciousness being remembered.

This change is energetic, emotional, physical, and spiritual.

This change can feel gentle at times. And uncomfortable at times.

This change is rapid in its speed. There is an acceleration to your experience now that will continue to grow exponentially.

Uncertainty and change are sometimes difficult. Every aspect of your life appears to be in flux now.

This does not mean that it is a negative experience. It is also opening your heart. It is also opening your intuition.

This experience is changing your perceptions of everything in your life.

Allow yourself to wait until you have full clarity before making major decisions.

This is a time of waiting, allowing, unfolding.

This is a time of faith, softness, and love.

This is tentative emergence, a gentle blossoming, and at times, a birthing through chaos.

We are here to assist you now. This is a major experience, and you are not alone.

If you need further support, we remind you to seek help and will always guide you to the right person for you. You will know who it is, as it will feel right in your heart.

Invocation

Angels, please guide me to the sacred healer, guide, wayshower, mentor or teacher that I have a soul contract to work with now.

Guiding Angels: Archangel Chamuel, Archangel Faith

DAY 142

Channelled Angel message

Take it slowly now. Have patience and faith. Learning to trust your heart guidance will take some time to adjust to.

Opening to your intuition and our guidance is indeed a leap of faith.

With so much change underway now, it is also important to honour your own journey.

We remind you that everything happens exactly when it is meant to. There truly is no need to push, force or rush.

Allowing is powerful. Allowing is abundant. Allowing is an act of self-love.

It also gives you space to adjust, test the waters, make mistakes, find your clarity, and listen to your inner knowing.

Allowing will feel uncomfortable at times. Faith will feel uncomfortable at times. This is the pathway of miracles.

You are learning/remembering a new way. One that is guided by your own heart, and that voice lies within. You know this way. You have prior knowledge from your higher soul consciousness of this way.

Create some space around you now. Allow yourself the opportunity to curiously feel your way through this journey.

Guidance is always available to you, from us, and from others when you need it.

And, from you. Your heart knows the way.

──────── Invocation ────────

Angels, please help me trust my heart guidance above all other voices now.

Guiding Angels: Archangel Michael, Archangel Haniel

DAY 143

Angel lesson: Archangel Butyalil

Archangel Butyalil is the Archangel of universal consciousness and the light of creation.

Archangel Butyalil is assisting humanity with realising a new understanding of the divine masculine, for both men and women.

Working with Archangel Butyalil in this area is fascinating and exciting, as he can guide you to experience a brand new, healed, and whole expression of the divine masculine that is as yet unknown and unexperienced here on Earth.

Many men will be anchoring this energy now, and there are many who have agreed to be wayshowers of this new expression of masculinity.

Equally, many women will be opening to a new experience and understanding of the divine masculine, which will require a miraculous shift in beliefs and ideas of the divine masculine.

This shift cannot happen unless it is experienced in balance.

This shift will transform relationships as we know them.

Archangel Butyalil is the Archangel of the stars and universe, of cosmic light and creation energy.

Anything can be created with light.

Anything can be healed with light.

Anything can be dismantled with light.

Anything that has dark energy and is no longer part of your purpose or contract can be uncreated, dismantled or removed with the assistance and cosmic light of Archangel Butyalil.

Archangel Butyalil can atomise or explode all artificial constructs, all illusions, all deceptions, all veils, all intentional blocks, and all matrix energy that is no longer needed.

Archangel Butyalil can atomise with his light of the cosmos all old energy that resides in your physical and energy body. If you are ready to upgrade and release an old pattern, belief, experience, system, or karmic contract, he can use sacred geometry to clear your physical and energy body to a DNA/cellular level. This process is only possible once all related karmic and soul lessons have been completed. Once you have full understanding of the lesson for all people involved, the upgrade and light healing can occur.

—————— Invocation ——————

Archangel Butyalil, I invite you to surround my being with the cosmic light of creation, clearing all distortions, illusions, cords, and dark vibrations. I ask to be reminded of my truth, to see clearly all that is hidden, and to expand my energy to its full potential now and ongoing. I am willing and ready to receive the new light codes for 5D consciousness through my experience and expression.

Guiding Angels: Archangel Butyalil
Energy: Masculine
Aura colour: Deep blue, gold, white

DAY 144

Channelled Angel message

As your heart and mind open now, we remind you to play and have fun.

As your heart attunes to the new love frequencies, we want to remind you that that love is joy, light is joy, and creation is joy.

As your heart chakra opens now, you will notice love all around you and within you. This will come in waves.

Sometimes you will feel heavy, sad, or overcome with grief for all that you did not see, the pain you turned a blind eye to, and the unexpressed grief within your heart. For some, this may even physically hurt as your heart chakra stretches and opens.

Sometimes you will feel loving, passionate, and deeply connected to those you love and are close to. You will feel deeply grateful for friendships, children, partners and everyone you love.

Sometimes you will feel elated, joyful, playful, childlike, and happy!

We remind you that joy is a part of your natural state of being.

We remind you that the more you allow yourself full expression of all your emotions, the more love and light will anchor through your light body and physical body—for as you notice and release grief, you make space for joy.

Joy, play, and laughter are ways the light is expressed through you in a raw, unfiltered way.

As you move through this shift now, we remind you to consciously choose activities that allow you to have fun, be playful and express your joy.

———— Invocation ————

Angels, please remind me to create joyful experiences as I move through this tremendous shift so that I can balance and integrate all light and darkness within.

Guiding Angels: Archangel Jophiel

DAY 145

Channelled Angel message

Your heart always knows the answer, and you are safe to trust it.

You are experiencing a heart shift.

Your heart is opening and expanding, along with your whole

energy body.

You are attuning to the new frequencies.

Love and light are flooding through you at levels you have not experienced in this lifetime, or any other earthly lifetime.

Your higher self, your soul, remembers this energy.

Your heart knows far more than your mind recalls just yet (this will change as you adjust to the new frequencies).

Your heart responds energetically to that which is aligned with love, and your highest good. When your heart responds, notice that. Follow that. This will guide you well with all decisions.

As you attune to the new frequencies and listen to your heart guidance, you might feel some discomfort as you begin to make different decisions, as you begin to trust yourself.

You will realise that you have never needed to seek the answer outside of yourself.

Those who guide you well will always listen and reflect your own wisdom back to you.

Your heart is an energetic receiver and transmitter of love.

You are far more powerful than you realise, and the power of love flowing through you now is awakening you to that memory and that truth.

Trust your heart guidance now. Let love guide you.

———————— Invocation ————————

Angels, please help me move through these energetic shifts and adjust to living from a new loving consciousness now.

Guiding Angels:
Archangel Metatron, Archangel Chamuel,
Archangel Nathaniel

DAY 146

Channelled Angel message

Take time to acknowledge your shifts, your progress, and your work.

The waves of frequency shifts now are taking you on a powerful journey.

Many of you will be experiencing rapid shifts and awakenings.

We remind you to pause and take a moment to acknowledge the sacred journey you are experiencing.

This is a beautiful blossoming, individually and collectively.

Your journey, Gaia's journey, and the journey of the collective are all interlinked.

You have come so far so quickly. Please take a moment to look at the significant shifts that you have experienced already this year. These seem subtle, and yet they are incredibly powerful.

Your relationships have changed.

Your sense of self has changed.

Your perception has changed.

You are speaking up, saying no, following your passion, expressing your feelings and trusting your intuition.

You are becoming the creator of your reality now.

Today, breathe into acknowledgement of your work and your progress. And then continue inwards and onwards, and let love guide you as always in all things.

———— Invocation ————

Angels, I feel your love surrounding me, uplifting me, reminding me of how far I've come, and that I am exactly where I am meant to be. I am not missing anything; I am not blocked; all is in divine perfect order.

DAY 147

Channelled Angel message

You are in transition now. The time in between. Honour this space, for it is as sacred as the beginning and the ending.

There is a sacred moment between what was and what will be.

There is energetic creation exploding all around you now in this transition place.

You are processing awareness of the endings. The lessons. The last healing remnants and shifts. This is incomplete. Honour the endings now.

You are seeding the beginnings, growing the visions and the feelings, building foundations for the new way, the new you, the new world. Honour the beginnings now.

This in-between stage is significant.

Do not rush or push now. Lean into the uncertainty and allow yourself to feel the energy in the tension held now.

Allow this shift to unfold at the pace that it requires, as it will unfold in divine timing regardless—for, as always, you truly have no control over this sacred birthing.

This is a miracle in the making.

Let go and allow it to unfold.

——————— Invocation ———————

Angels, please remind me that at times when I feel the most discomfort, tension, and uncertainty, I am in the midst of a miracle unfolding, and to let go and allow it to play in perfect divine timing.

DAY 148

Channelled Angel message

We invite you to be curious about truth as you understand it now. Be gentle with yourself as you see new perspectives.

There is a collective theme of truths being revealed now.

You are experiencing this within your own self-awareness, as well as with how you relate to others, and to your community and the wider collective.

We ask you to notice, to be curious and discerning with personal and collective beliefs, and what you understand to be true.

We invite you to investigate gently those beliefs you have held as true always.

We ask you to be gentle and compassionate with yourself as truth is revealed to you. And to allow yourself space and time to process this stage of your awakening journey.

We remind you that this process will continue, that this is not a one-time awareness shift.

As your vibration raises, and you attune to the new frequencies, you will open more to see through the veil.

At times, this might feel confusing and unsettling. At times, it might trigger shame, grief, anger, and rage.

You are safe and protected.

Go gently now through this stage of your awakening.

Remember to ask for support from the divine and your Angelic team.

You are loved dearly.

Your process is one of power returning to you.

You are a powerful light being, and you are reclaiming your connection to source/the creator now.

This is a sacred journey, and we are with you.

—————— Invocation ——————

Angels, please help me find compassion for self and others as I now see my own and the collective shadows.

Guiding Angels:
Archangel Zadkiel, Archangel Haniel, Archangel Grace

DAY 149

There is a new cycle beginning now.

There is a softness anchoring now.

Change will continue, but today we ask you to notice the work you have done, how far you have come, and the change you have created.

Honour your progress. See the immense growth. See the love blossoming within your heart.

This is still the transition. However, you are now anchored more fully into your next cycle, and this cycle is one that is immersed in love and guided by your heart.

This is about being guided by love in all things.

This cycle is only just emerging into form.

This is not a time to act, rather it is a time to be cautious, discerning, open and curious.

This is a heart blossoming into the new world.

You are the heart that is blossoming. You are safe to open your heart to this new cycle.

Angels, please help me anchor into my newly found open hearted expression of consciousness. Help me feel love for myself and all beings.

Guiding Angels:
Archangel Chamuel, Archangel Nathaniel, Archangel Grace

DAY 150

Channelled Angel message

You came here for a reason. It is time to awaken to your mission now.

The great awakening is here.

You have a mission to serve the light.

You are not here now by chance. You have many lifetimes of work in the light, and you chose to be here now to support the great shift that is underway.

You are a lightworker, a light healer, a light activator, a light leader, a light lover, a light teacher, a light rebel, a light warrior or all or some of these at once.

Your mission is a full expression of your authentic self.

Everything that you have experienced until now was to help you awaken to your purpose and mission.

Right now, you are experiencing a mission activation, calling you to step further into expression of your purpose.

You are expanding and awakening to a deeper expression of your true self now.

*Angels, please show me my next step so that I may recall my
mission and be of service now.*

Guiding Angels: Archangel Michael, Archangel Nathaniel

DAY 151

Angel lesson: Archangel Metatron

Archangel Metatron is the Angel of Ascension. He is helping
anchor the new 5D earth energies, works with sacred geometry,
and supports all star-children and their families.

Archangel Metatron feels huge, expansive, comforting and
grounding. Because he works so much with energy and frequency,
his vibration can often feel both intense and grounding.

Archangel Metatron assists all lightworkers and healers and
all humans with acclimatising to the new 5D frequencies.

Archangel Metatron does additional work with some
lightworkers and light leaders who have a soul contract to work
on the earth frequencies and anchor the new light (ascension
guides).

Archangel Metatron works with sacred geometry as a healing
expression of the light of creation.

Archangel Metatron helps indigos, rainbow children, crystal
children and all other star children adjust to the earth experience.
He also assists parents of these special children.

———— Invocation ————

*Archangel Metatron, please help me hear your guidance so that I
can experience my own ascension journey smoothly and support*

those around me in the capacity that I am guided to (whether that be as a light leader, lightworker, or parent or carer of the children of the light).

Guiding Angel: Archangel Metatron
Energy: Masculine
Aura colour: Green & violet

DAY 152

Channelled Angel message

Your highest priority now is to receive and share light and love.

We see you sometimes despair at the darkness in your life now, in your world now.

And we remind you that the darkness has always been there.

It is becoming visible now and will become more so.

The veil is thinning.

Your third eye is opening.

You are experiencing an awakening to truth, to new perspectives, and your higher consciousness.

At times, this is joyful, as your heart remembers that divine love is available to you.

At times, this is deeply painful, as you experience grief for loss of self and grief for the world.

Both are occurring. Both are appropriate.

There is a great need for the light to shine now, and your role is not just important—it is vital.

There are many ways you can contribute.

Focus on your own ascension journey, your own spiritual awakening, and receive the new light frequencies in your own heart. If this is all you can do now, it is both enough and vital.

We ask you to share the light however you can. Speak with

love. Act with love. Bring truth and light to darkness through your own being. Hold love and compassion. Be love and compassion.

Step into service of the light now.

Your path is divinely guided.

———— Invocation ————

Angels, please remind me that my own awakening and ascension is all I need focus on now.

Guiding Angels:
Archangel Faith, Archangel Haniel, Archangel Metatron

DAY 153

Channelled Angel message

This is a sensitive time. Go gently, with yourself and others around you.

We remind you that as the veil lifts, as your energy attunes to the higher love frequencies, your sensitivity will increase.

With each wave of frequency shift, you will experience a settling period.

All humans will react differently to these shifts.

For some, this will trigger wounding, shadow healing, and pain. This may translate as anger, rage or grief.

For others, this will invoke a deep passion to create change.

For some, it will bring waves of hope, love, and inspiration to be of service.

At times, you might oscillate between all these experiences in waves.

Remember that your heart is opening now and adjusting to feeling more.

So today, we remind you to see the big picture, and to go gently.

Now is a time for love, compassion, forgiveness, kindness, and soft words.

It is a time for patience, detachment, and empathy.

It is a time to see your own shadow and be self-loving.

This is what opening to love feels like. It is blissful at times, and it is painful at times, and you will settle into this new, deeper experience of connection to all living beings.

———————— Invocation ————————

Angels, please remind me that the intensity of the feelings I am experiencing is a natural part of my awakening and ascension journey.

Guiding Angels:
Archangel Zadkiel, Archangel Chamuel, Archangel Metatron

DAY 154

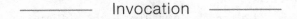

Channelled Angel message

You are receiving powerful new love/light frequencies now.

The ascension of Gaia and her inhabitants is underway.

Gaia is moving from a third density (3D) frequency to a 5D frequency.

The last time Gaia underwent a shift like this was in the time of Atlantis.

5D frequency was not fully anchored at that time, and humanity cycled back into 3rd density. This ascension cycle is occurring again now.

As the light frequency increases, your vibration changes. As the veil of fear and separation lifts, and you clearly see all that was hidden within and without.

The darkness that was always there is being exposed now.

As you awaken to your own shadows and veils, you also see the collective shadows and veils.

This process is a deep healing and transformation, and at times can feel overwhelming, painful, and hard to witness.

We remind you that New Earth is birthing through this process and through you.

Find and express the vision of New Earth that you see within your own heart now.

This is not a time for war. That is the old way. New Earth energies are peaceful and founded in compassion, forgiveness, acceptance, and unconditional love.

Access and integrate the 5D light frequencies in nature. Place your body on the earth to allow Gaia to attune your energy to the Gaia frequency.

You will feel your energy soften when you experience regular attunement with Gaia. The great shift will feel easier.

This is vital for your process now.

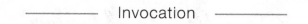

Invocation

Angels, please remind me to spend time in nature to become attuned to the new, loving, and peaceful frequencies that are activating within my mind, body, and spirit now.

Guiding Angels:
Archangel Gaia, Archangel Gersisa, Archangel Metatron

DAY 155

Channelled Angel message

Become aware of everything that brings you joy and do that now. Anchor the light now.

The ascension of Gaia and all life is accelerating.

This is creating turbulence as many cling to old beliefs and structures, or react to pain points.

Practise compassion and acceptance as you witness this process, and trust that all will happen as it is meant to.

Practise compassion and acceptance for yourself as you also at times react to your pain points and triggers.

The great awakening brings vision and clarity to all. At first, this awareness feels difficult. And then love guides the way to hope for and faith in a new way.

The new world is being imagined now.

In order for it to birth, the collective consciousness must evolve to a 5D expression. This will occur when humanity reaches a collective mass of love and light. Unity.

This process is accelerating now.

Your part is vital. Your ability to hold and share the light creates a wave of exponential light frequencies.

To do this, focus on your own ascension.

Raise your vibration now by being, and doing, everything that is your light practice. Everything that is a full soul expression of love for you. Everything that is your unfiltered expression of joy, light and love.

Be you. Express you. Rebel in the process of being you now.

Love all that you are like never before.

Make radical choices to reject fear and old broadcasts of outdated beliefs, ideologies, habits, and structures. They are falling around you and within you faster than you can imagine.

Be love now.

Angels, please assist me through my own process of bringing shadows to light and moving into a higher awareness.

Guiding Angels:
Archangel Haniel, Archangel Metatron, Archangel Michael

DAY 156

Channelled Angel message

There really is nothing to fear.

We remind you to notice that when you are in nature, your heart remembers that you are safe, and that everything is ok.

We remind you to notice that when you first wake, there is a time when your heart is connected to the divine source, and you feel peace.

We remind you to feel that energy now, that peaceful place of knowing, of sovereignty.

There really is nothing to fear. There never was.

We invite you to remember that you have access to this peace always.

We ask you to let it grow, focus on it, let it radiate. Repeat it. Practise it.

There really is nothing to fear.

You are eternal.

All heals in the light in the end.

The pathway is bumpy and painful at times, and magical and miraculous also.

Allow yourself to let the fear pass and wash away now.

And what is left is hope, acceptance, compassion, peace, and forgiveness.

Let go. Soften. Breathe into the peace that you feel when you find this space.

——————— Invocation ———————

Angels, please help me let go of fear and remember that I am eternal, and safe.

Guiding Angels: Archangel Michael, Archangel Faith

DAY 157

Channelled Angel message

As we transition to New Earth, know that your reality helps create the collective reality.

There is a miraculous process of transformation underway now.

As Gaia ascends to 5D, so do you.

As change erupts around you, it also does within your own micro world.

We ask you to notice the rapid rate of change now.

We invite you to open to the idea that everything that was fixed and certain is now in flux.

The new earth will operate from a different vibration. One that does not yet exist and has not fully birthed.

Your experience of change now will help anchor this new vibration.

And so, we ask you to anchor to love now.

Anchor on love rather than the past that is evaporating, rather than the collective response, rather than a fear response.

Witness and experience the transition from a place of detachment, compassion, love, and curiosity.

The process is incomplete.
Allow it to unfold and blossom.

—————— Invocation ——————

Angels, please remind me to stay present and embody the change that is occurring now.

Guiding Angels:
Archangel Nathaniel, Archangel Faith, Archangel Grace

DAY 158

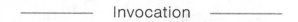
Channelled Angel message

We see the effort that you are making to embody love now.

We see that you are self-enquiring now.

We see that you are practising forgiveness, compassion, acceptance, and unconditional love.

We see that you are noticing your own beliefs and questioning them when they are judgemental, unloving, outdated, or creating separation from others.

This process might feel uncomfortable and challenging at times.

We notice that you are expressing your feelings and opinions from a place of loving acceptance and forgiveness.

We notice that sometimes you feel angry, sad, confused and even ashamed through this process.

We offer confirmation that this is the pathway.

We remind you that the more you look at things from a perspective of love, the more love anchors on Earth now.

We remind you that light and love are anchoring on Earth faster than ever before. You are helping create a new vibration.

Your heart chakra is activating and opening now.
We see you radiating love now.
You are not alone. You are becoming the light now.

Invocation

Angels, please give me clear signs that I am on the right path now as I confront my shadows and embody the 5D frequency asking to be expressed through me now.

Guiding Angels:
Archangel Chamuel, Archangel Metatron,
Archangel Nathaniel

DAY 159

Channelled Angel message

If you had no more time, what would you do? Who would you love?

Do that now.

As you experience your great shift and awakening now, you may feel untethered at times.

As 'all that was' shifts to 'all that will be', we ask you to get clear on what and who you love. And follow that with devotion like never before.

There is a magical energy of creation unfolding in your life and in the collective now.

Everything is possible if you can follow love.

If you want to experience exponential growth now, we invite you to trust and love like never before.

*Angels, please show me the pathway that is my
expression of love now.*

Guiding Angels: Archangel Chamuel, Archangel Faith

DAY 160

Channelled Angel message

You are blossoming now. Allow the process to unfold. You do not
need to push.

This part of your journey has an inevitability.

Your destiny awaits you; it always did.

Truthfully, there is nothing you need to force or push. What
will be will be, in divine timing and for the highest good of you
and all others involved.

Your intuitive guidance is strong, and you are being asked to
have faith and allow this sacred journey to unfold before you.

For this part of your journey is truly sacred and magical.

Look around you. Healing is occurring. Love is blossoming.
Miracles are seeding.

There is a rebirth occurring now.

You are emerging and you are about to welcome a new cycle
of life.

As is Gaia.

Have faith now as you experience and witness the unfolding.
Allow yourself to feel it and be present for this important shift.

—————— Invocation ——————

*Angels, please remind me to stay present and allow myself to
experience this miraculous shift.*

DAY 161

Channelled Angel message

Trust your truth. No other knows your path, and your guidance is true.

We remind you to clear your energy field of deception, and the influence of others and the collective energy.

You are a highly intuitive, sovereign being, and your own truth is powerful and clear.

It is always there. You need only ask to be shown the truth as it exists for you, and you will be guided with clear signs, messages, feelings, or knowing's.

On this journey, you will reclaim your power, your voice, and your expression of your unique self.

We remind you to shine, to speak up and express all parts of your dear unique self, without self-judgement or criticism.

Now more than ever, the world needs your light, your vision, your humour, your wisdom, and your voice!

Your purpose is to be you! Unashamedly.

Your purpose is to love being you! For you are wonderful and loveable, and your difference is your gift!

By radiating your truth now, you shine a path for others to follow.

─────── Invocation ───────

Angels, please help me see, feel, and express my full and truthful expression of self now.

Guiding Angels: Archangel Nathaniel, Archangel Michael

DAY 162

Channelled Angel message

Your purpose is to give and receive love. This is the reason you are here.

Every experience, every relationship, every interaction is to teach you about the experience of love.

Love is your reason for being. And the answer to every difficulty you might face.

As you awaken now collectively, the awakening experience brings you closer to love.

You are seeing all the ways that you and the collective have turned away from love.

You are craving a deeper experience of love.

Your emotions and connections feel deeper. Your whole awareness of the nature of love is shifting.

This is in direct correlation to the frequency shifts occurring. As Gaia and the human collective shift from 3D frequency to 5D frequency, you are able to experience, receive and express more love.

New Earth is anchored in love. Love is the way forward now.

The transition occurring is one of awareness and revelation.

All beings are experiencing a shift in consciousness, allowing for a deeper experience of love.

This is the shift. The transition period.

Love is the pathway through it.

———— Invocation ————

Angels, please show me all ways that I can open to a deeper experience of love now.

Guiding Angels: Archangel Chamuel, Archangel Faith

DAY 163

Channelled Angel message

Trust only your inner guidance now. Seek clarity in nature and listen to your heart.

As your intuition expands and opens now, you will begin to see new ways of living and being.

You will begin to receive guidance and new options all around you. The floodgates will open.

This can be both a wonderful blessing, and sometimes confusing and overwhelming. Self-doubt is normal, and you will become more confident trusting your heart as you practise this.

We remind you that your pathway is yours alone.

This does not mean that you won't receive guidance, assistance, advice and learning from outside sources. This is valuable and part of your purpose as you learn about love and interact with others.

However, not all sources know your path, and not all guidance is for you.

The path is always the one that feels right to you.

When you listen and act from your heart with integrity towards your own feelings and those of others, you will always choose correctly.

Your guidance is strong.

Your heart always knows the way forward.

Clarity comes exactly when it is meant to. If you do see the way forward, ask for guidance and wait. The next step will be revealed in divine timing, and you will know it in your heart.

———————— Invocation ————————

Angels, please help me practise trusting my own intuition and guidance above all other voices now. Please help me sit in the discomfort of not knowing and remind me that clarity will come.

Guiding Angels:
Archangel Haniel, Archangel Michael, Archangel Faith

DAY 164

Channelled Angel message

Faith is your heart showing you the way forwards.

Your intuition is your body responding to the vibration of love. It speaks to you in many ways and opens you to our guidance.

One of the first and strongest ways your intuition guides you is via your heart.

Your heart is an energetic instrument that responds to everything it interacts with. This is true for all dimensions and times.

Your heart connects your energy system to source, to your origin, to the divine, to us.

Your heart responds to all that it interacts with, in past, present, and future time.

Your heart can create the future. Your positive reaction to something you imagine can have such a powerful impact on you that your choices and actions create that future event.

This is manifestation, creation, and miracles in action.

Love is the energy of creation.

Hope is the seed of miracles.

———— Invocation ————

Angels, please remind me that my greatest power is my capacity to love, feel, and imagine. I am the creator. Please help me have faith now.

Guiding Angels:
Archangel Chamuel, Archangel Ariel, Archangel Faith

DAY 165

Channelled Angel message

The new earth energy is unconditional love, compassion, forgiveness, and acceptance. This is unity consciousness. Embody this now.

As the veil lifts and the world awakens, you will experience shifts of clarity and vision.

Wounds are being triggered now, individually, and collectively for swift integration and healing.

The rate of change, awakening and ascension is rapid and compounding.

All that comes to the surface can be swiftly healed and cleared in all dimensions now, in order to break the chains of darkness and open the pathway for the new world to birth.

For your part in this, we ask you to focus on your own truth, your own healing, and allowing your own shifts in consciousness. This assists the collective to bring forth the best possible outcome for all humanity.

Allow the light to move through you, embody love, embody acceptance, allow yourself to be healed, embody unity, embody 5D.

Set a pathway for those around you to see a new way.

Become a beacon of light now.

You may notice circuits breaking and new pathways opening in your own life at a rapid pace now.

You assist the collective experience by doing your own ascension work.

The ascension of Gaia to 5D and New Earth is inevitable.

Angels, please remind me that I assist the collective shift in consciousness when I experience my own shift in consciousness.

Guiding Angels: Archangel Metatron

DAY 166

Channelled Angel message

You are receiving new light codes. Make space to integrate them.

As the vibration of Gaia shifts further to 5D (love/light and unity consciousness), so do you.

Light is flooding Earth now, encoded with information from source.

Each of you has your own ascension journey.

All you need to do is follow your heart; it will guide you now.

Specific light codes are anchoring now to prepare you for service to the collective.

Your self-care, light practice and light work are your vehicle to discovering this mission.

Your own inner light practice is the foundation for your light work.

The new light codes activate recall of information from your Akashic record of prior incarnations, and you will consciously recall this information in divine timing.

Pure water and foods, rest, and movement are all important parts of your integration of new light codes now, as is your advancement of your own light practice.

The shift is escalating and your activation to service occurs now.

Angels, please guide me clearly to the highest priority for embodiment of my destined path and recall of my mission.

Guiding Angels: Archangel Michael, Archangel Metatron

DAY 167

Channelled Angel message

New timelines are always seeding. All outcomes are possible. That which you hope for already exists in a future/now reality.

We remind you to have deep faith now.

Practise awareness of your emotional body and notice your fears. Are you experiencing an energetic reaction to the collective? Is this also part of your own experience?

Are your beliefs about what is happening, and what is possible, true? What shifts when you become curious about what is happening and what is possible?

What else exists now in your experience that you are not seeing? What else is possible and anchoring now?

All outcomes are possible.

All that you hope for exists.

Practise imagining the experience that you wish for, so that your heart has a true feeling of that vision.

This is alchemy. This is heart magic. This is creation.

Your love is your anchor to the new world. Your heart is both a magnet and a creator.

Love, curiosity, and imagination are your greatest powers now.

Angels, please help me feel, see, and imagine my highest timeline
so that I can create and actualise it now.

Guiding Angels:
Archangel Haniel, Archangel Faith, Archangel Ariel

DAY 168

Channelled Angel message

This is the most important time of your life. Of any lifetime.

Everything is changing now. For you and all humanity.

The great awakening has become an event that has created a new timeline.

You are now shifting between two cycles, two timelines, two realities. The old 3D experience still holds your blueprint and physicality. The new 5D world is beginning to anchor through your consciousness, and your energy is shifting between the two realities.

This presents as miraculous shifts of understanding of what is possible, what is real, and how to love.

This is the transition, death, and creation phase.

Death of old ways. Death of old beliefs. Death of old self.

Birth of a new world.

Birth of a new you.

Be patient. You are in the fire. Hold faith and embody love.

You are surrounded and supported by your Angelic team.

You chose to be here now for this very experience.

It is a sacred journey, and your role is important.

Angels, please remind me that the transition time is occurring now, and that it is normal to experience a sense of two realities. Please help me navigate this time in a way that is in alignment with my highest pathway.

Guiding Angels: Archangel Faith, Archangel Nathaniel, Archangel Metatron

DAY 169

Channelled Angel message

There is a new pathway emerging for you now. This is a heart journey. Trust your heart.

Your pathway might feel as if it's a leap of faith. It is.

You might feel as if you are the only one who understands your pathway. You are.

You might feel as if you cannot see the future. You can't.

This is a brand-new pathway.

You have not taken this pathway in this lifetime, or in any other.

This pathway is one being created by love, faith, and imagination.

You do not walk this pathway alone.

You have loving support around you. Friends. Mentors. Family. Loved ones.

Mother Gaia and all plants and animals support you on this journey.

And you have us. There are infinite Angelic beings of light guiding you, encouraging you and cheering you on.

Your guidance is true. Your heart is not leading you astray.

Trust the whispers, the feelings and the guidance that are presenting before you now.

It has never been more important for you to follow your heart. Not just for yourself, but for the collective human experience.

Each one of you who anchors and trusts the pathway of a love helps create a new earth reality now.

―――――――― Invocation ――――――――

Angels, please help me trust and embody the pathway of love as it appears before me now, even if no other understands it.

Guiding Angels:
Archangel Michael, Archangel Faith, Archangel Metatron

DAY 170

Channelled Angel message

The change you desire is birthing now.

Perhaps you feel as if you need to take action to push through the discomfort you feel.

Perhaps you feel as if this is something you can control.

Perhaps you feel like you've had enough of waiting. Like it's not fair.

Perhaps you feel like you've had faith, and it hasn't worked.

This feeling is the surrender moment.

The discomfort will seem unbearable right before the moment when you experience a tremendous breakthrough, a miracle. A brand-new experience and a brand-new world.

What you seek exists. You are moving towards it as fast as it is moving towards you.

There is no need to push. Pushing is a form of resistance and will not speed this process; in fact, it could extend or delay it.

This is a process of trust, allowing and acceptance.

It is a process of faith and trusting your heart.

Your heart knows the way forward here.

New Earth is made up of new you. New you does things you have never done before.

Begin now.

Wait. Breathe through the final stages and allow the birthing.

Let go and surrender to the new experience waiting for you now.

─────── Invocation ───────

Angels, please help me move through the discomfort of the moment before surrender and remind me to soften and let go.

Guiding Angels:
Archangel Faith, Archangel Nathaniel, Archangel Metatron

DAY 171

Channelled Angel message

You are creating a new pathway now.

Linear time does not exist. All times exist at once.

Now is all that matters.

The old 3D way of goal setting, hard work, constant action and never enough time is shifting and crumbling now.

The 5D pathway is emerging now and is one of faith, abundance, plenty and flow.

Action is still required, but balance and harmony and energetic alignment are now more powerful than unconscious force and continual action.

Everything you understand about abundance, creation,

prosperity, and success is up for questioning now. All are being re-imagined and rebirthed now as the collective anchors 5D New Earth.

You have an opportunity now to create from a brand-new place, with limitless potential.

Allow yourself to be guided now by inspiration, integrity, authentic self-expression, and the natural ebbs and flows of your own energy.

Everything created from this new energy will naturally and powerfully attract success, and will also feel easier, more enjoyable, and peaceful as you are following your natural rhythms and inspiration.

This is a potent time of collective innovation, creation, and reinvention. Opportunity is everywhere and will be divinely inspired and heart created.

————— Invocation —————

Angels, please help me flow with the new pathway of abundance, creation and success that is divinely inspired, and heart guided now.

Guiding Angels:
Archangel Haniel, Archangel Ariel, Archangel Faith

DAY 172

Channelled Angel message

There are miracles unfolding all around you now.

Slow down to see and feel them.

Be mindful of your pace now. There is much urgency and distraction in the collective.

Look here! Be afraid!

Look there! Work harder!

There is always enough time. The earth provides for all in abundance and plenty.

As you slow your breath and soften into the present moment, you will feel and hear our loving guidance more easily.

And then, around you, the miracles will begin to unfold.

It is in flow with the energy of love, creation and the divine that you find the new way, the new earth, the way of love.

Faith is the gateway. Surrender is the path.

We whisper guidance with rainbows and clouds, music, and wind.

Curiosity will create serendipitous moments that surprise you.

The small moments and miracles open your heart to greater ones. The rainbow, sunrise and blossom remind you that all miracles are equal, that you are a miracle, and that you are opening to miracles now.

Trust your heart, slow down and breathe into the present moment now.

─────── Invocation ───────

Angels, please help me slow down and pause to see and feel the miracles that already exist in my world.

Guiding Angels:
Archangel Uriel, Archangel Faith, Archangel Michael

DAY 173

Channelled Angel message

You are on the right track. Keep following your heart now.

Your consciousness expands in direct proportion to the rate

that your heart opens.

Your heart is your connection to all that you desire.

Your heart is the instrument that creates, that feels, that guides, that manifests, that heals, and that connects you to us and to all living beings.

Everything you do that is heart guided now helps change your experience and anchor the new 5D reality.

Heart guidance is accepting, unifying, abundant, healing and connective.

Living from your heart is as simple as allowing yourself to fully express all your emotions, desires, and inspiration.

Living from your heart is a remembering, and deeply healing.

Living from your heart is a reclamation of sovereignty and is your greatest power now.

———————— Invocation ————————

Angels, please help me through the process of opening my heart and living from my heart.

Guiding Angels:
Archangel Chamuel, Archangel Raphael, Archangel Zadkiel

DAY 174

Channelled Angel message

There is vast assistance and support available to you now.

You are not alone. And yet some days you may feel more alone than ever.

Your mission is to create a new pathway now and light the way for others who do not yet see the light. You are here now to help bring radical miraculous change.

This experience is why you chose to be here on Earth now.

Every person reading this has a role to play.

Your purpose is to follow your heart, awaken, and embody unconditional love.

Some days, this feels like an act of rebellion, anarchy, or war.

Remember that you are also experiencing an energetic interplay with the collective, so at times you will pick up on the collective fear mindset, and collective grief.

Even though you sometimes feel isolated, you are not.

Even though you feel different, wrong, alone, you are not.

Your rebellious and committed embodiment of the vibration of love is vital now.

And you have never been more supported.

By us, your Angels.

By your ancestors.

By sentient beings of light from other times, places, and dimensions.

By other lightworkers who serve a mission to support you now.

By mother Gaia and all plants and animals.

—————— Invocation ——————

Angels, please help me feel the infinite support from all beings who are here to assist me on my pathway now.

Guiding Angels: All Archangels and Guardian Angels

DAY 175

Channelled Angel message

You are not meant to see the future now. That would ruin the miracles along the way.

You are never meant to see the future.

Earth is an experience you choose to participate in, knowing that it is a series of miracles unfolding.

Each hurdle, challenge and difficulty have a lesson, blessing or reason. Not all are meant to be positive. Not all difficult experiences are negative.

You chose to be here now.

This time is indeed significant. Great change is underway for you, and for all.

A new experience of reality is birthing now. A new understanding of love, of life, of what is possible, of time, of abundance, of miracles and of healing.

All that births now does so through human consciousness.

Through you.

All that is birthing now is being imagined and created through you.

The change that occurs will be inspired, imagined, and dreamed.

Your passion, anger, grief, confusion, and pain will all alchemise into creative form.

You are the conduit, you are the channel you are the miracle.

——————— Invocation ———————

Angels, please remind me to let go of desire to see and control my future so that I can be in this moment and experience divinely inspired creation now.

Guiding Angels:
Archangel Faith, Archangel Haniel, Archangel Metatron

DAY 176

Channelled Angel message

There is always time to pause before the next frequency shift.

You will receive guidance and clarity on your next steps at the exact right time. This is a time to rest, adjust, acclimatise and be in the moment.

There is no rush.

You are growing rapidly.

Take time now just to be and to enjoy this place before the next wave and expansion.

This can be a fun process. Laugh now, be with friends and family, spend time outdoors and doing activities that help you radiate love and happiness.

Each frequency shift brings a new energy and awareness, and your body/mind/spirit needs time to adjust and integrate. This is such a time.

Listen to the messages your body is giving you now. Be mindful of how you fuel your body, rest, and move.

Nature will be wonderful for you now, as always.

Have fun in this space in between.

———————— Invocation ————————

Angels, please help me sit in the tension of the time in between. Please help me be present to this time of inspiration and integration now.

Guiding Angels:
Archangel Nathaniel, Archangel Faith, Archangel Metatron

DAY 177

Channelled Angel message

All you need to do is love. It is the answer to and reason for everything. And now is the time to love with abandon.

Love is the energy that creates all that you desire.

Love is the energy of all creation, of the divine, of miracles, of life.

Any area in your life that is causing you pain or suffering can be made easier or transformed with love.

Love will lead you to your mission and purpose.

Love activates all healing.

Love is a vibration, and every action made with love as its guide has an impact on the collective consciousness.

The collective consciousness is experiencing the most significant shift in human history now.

This shift is an awakening, and love is the gateway and path through this awakening.

Embodying unconditional love is your highest priority right now.

Invocation

Angels, please help me open my heart so that I feel safe giving and receiving love. Please help me trust my heart guidance now.

Guiding Angels:
Archangel Chamuel, Archangel Michael, Archangel Faith

DAY 178

Channelled Angel message

Love is everywhere when you look for it.

Love is an energy that exists in all living things.

Love is there for you to feel and receive every day.

When you are seeking love, we invite you to begin to focus on where love already exists in your life.

Love is in music.

Love is in the sunrise and sunset.

Love is in friendship.

Love is in family.

Love is in the birds, the clouds, the wind, and the rain.

Love is in the family that you pass walking together.

Love is in the friends you see meeting to be together.

Love is in you.

As you seek love, we invite you to open your heart to appreciate where love already exists.

Your vibration gently shifts and attunes with love as you appreciate love.

As you become love, be love, embody love, notice, and appreciate love, you become that which you seek.

Love flows where love exists. Love exists everywhere as soon as you bring your awareness to it.

───────── Invocation ─────────

Angels, please help me see all the wonderful ways and places where love already exists in my life.

Guiding Angels: Archangel Chamuel, Archangel Jophiel

DAY 179

Channelled Angel message

As you begin to see the new world seed, take time to appreciate the journey.

The energy of appreciation is the energy of love.

Noticing your part in this journey is a powerful act of love.

Everything you live, breathe, and speak now is a creative force of love.

You are manifesting into form all that you desire, and all that exists in the new earth.

This is a miraculous time! A joyous time!

There is a beautiful balance of urgency and divine timing right now.

You need not push now. All is flowing to you with grace, and yet your desire to express yourself as all that you are feels vital. Urgent.

Breathe through this experience by focusing on all that you are, and all that you love!

You are a radiant being of love. A miracle in form.

 Invocation ————

Angels, please help me feel gratitude and appreciation for every aspect of my journey until now, as every experience has been in perfect divine order to make me who I am today.

Guiding Angels:
Archangel Jeremiel, Archangel Jophiel, Archangel Faith

DAY 180

Channelled Angel message

You are capable of far more than you realise. Ask to expand your next level now.

Truly, this is a marvellous time of expansion and light.

We ask you to be curious, playful, and open, and allow the divine to flow through you to a capacity that you can hold. Your potential is vast. And you are ready.

Whatever your capacity, wherever you feel your edge is, we invite you to let go and open to this next wave of light and growth.

This next wave will integrate gently and slowly. Trust your readiness to expand.

This next wave of light is one that will inspire you and bring clarity.

Laser-sharp vision awaits you in all areas of your life.

You are becoming and refining your expression of self, and this is integrating through all aspects of your mind/body/spirit.

Allow this experience to flow through you now.

———— Invocation ————

Angels, please help me trust and open to expanding to my full potential now. Please help me let go of all resistance and open to the light now.

Guiding Angels:
Archangel Faith, Archangel Michael, Archangel Metatron

DAY 181

Channelled Angel message

Your purpose is ascension. Love, service, and healing are the pathway.

You are here to awaken to the truth of your purpose, your mission.

Your mission is your gateway to service to the many.

Your journey to your mission requires you to heal your shadow, your trauma, your pain—to integrate your wounds and find compassion, healing and acceptance for yourself and others.

Your mission is predestined. You chose it before you incarnated.

Your challenges are your gifts. They are the clues to discovering your role through embodiment.

The pathway is guided by love. It is a heart experience, with faith and wondrous, joyous love available at every expansion.

It is not meant to be perfect. Ascension is still a human process. You will continue to learn along the way.

It need not be serious. In fact, the more you express all aspects of yourself, the more you will expand.

So have fun along the way. Be creative. Listen to music. Love. Laugh. Be with yourself in the moment.

This is your time to rise.

——————— Invocation ———————

Angels, please help me open to my own ascension journey now, without resistance. Please show me the way so that I can discover the next step on the journey to remembering my mission.

Guiding Angels:
Archangel Michael, Archangel Metatron, Archangel Faith

DAY 182

Channelled Angel message

You are safe to open your heart to the love you are feeling now.

Your ascension journey is one of love. Your heart chakra is activating now.

As you experience your next-level awakening, you are feeling deeper levels of connection to all living things.

The colours in the sky will feel and seem radiant now.

The wind on your cheeks will feel like a loving caress now.

You can feel love radiating from the birds as they sing their greetings with joy in their hearts.

Your children, partner, family and loved ones are connecting on deeper levels.

And, for some of you, your heart is seeking love with another.

The pathway to love is always inwards. The love that is activating in all areas of your life is the pathway to love with another.

You can practise opening your heart with all you interact with. And this will blossom into an open connection with the one you are seeking, who is also seeking you.

You are safe to experience this deepening connection of love.

─────── Invocation ───────

Angels, please help me open to deeper experiences of love in all areas of my life now.

Guiding Angels: Archangel Chamuel

DAY 183

Channelled Angel message

The miracles you seek come in divine perfect timing. Have faith.

There is a wonder to miracles. They require faith, detachment and for things to play out with a timing and order that benefit all involved.

Remember that there is perfection in every meeting, experience, and outcome.

Things happen for reasons we do not understand; even the painful experiences have meaning.

If you are seeking a miracle, we assure you that it has been heard, and that the wheels are in motion.

Your part is to listen, flow, and be open to the divine.

The divine speaks to you in every breath, and the guidance through this experience is there for you when you ask and open to receive it.

But first, you must let go of all resistance, and surrender.

Surrendering control allows the energy to flow to you in the space that is created when you let go.

The outcome is better than you can imagine. Let go now and allow it to flow to you in divine timing.

———— Invocation ————

Angels, please help me let go of all resistance so that I can trust in divine timing and open to miracles now.

Guiding Angels:
Archangel Faith, Archangel Michael, Archangel Ariel

DAY 184

Channelled Angel message

All discomfort is a message.

When you feel afraid, we want to remind you that you are not alone.

When you feel uncertain, we want to remind you that the unknown is not unsafe.

When you feel as if you may be hurt, and want to protect your heart, we want to remind you that love is the reason for living.

When you feel attached, and need to control your situation, we want to remind you that miracles require surrender and flow.

Discomfort passes.

Discomfort is human.

When you notice yourself feeling discomfort, we invite you to work with us.

There is guidance available to you here, and your experience is a meaningful part of your journey.

Become curious when you feel discomfort. It is your intuition asking you to look sideways rather than ahead or behind. What is here for you to explore? What are you missing? What remains unhealed? What can you accept, forgive, learn from, let go of, or be present to?

This is the purpose. The journey is the purpose.

Your body is a finely tuned energetic being that has indicators that can guide you through your experiences. And you can work with these feelings as a map to your human experience, evolution, growth, and ascension.

——————— Invocation ———————

Angels, please help me see my discomfort as a message and gateway to growth. Please remind me in the moment that every situation is here to teach me something and is in divine perfect order for my growth.

Guiding Angels: Archangel Faith, Archangel Metatron

DAY 185

Channelled Angel message

Everything will become clear at the right time. Have faith.

We know that many of you who have future sight cannot see the future clearly now.

We want to explain this process.

A miraculous event is unfolding now.

Your ability to see and interact with future timelines is changing now, and your vision is shifting from linear to quantum.

Timelines now will not become fully clear until the moment right before they anchor or actualise. Until this occurs, probability will be fluid and in flux. It will be impossible to see the future with clarity.

Your collective consciousness is changing and is now able to interact with future timelines, with probability and with creation in a new way now.

This is part of the journey to New Earth.

In order for the highest possible timeline to anchor, you will need to practise detachment, faith, and acceptance of the free will of all beings.

There are no mistakes. Everything happens in perfect divine timing.

All will be revealed in time. There is an integrity to this process that cannot be violated lest it impacts the outcome of all concerned.

Trust that you will be shown your next step at the right time, and that the highest timeline for the wellbeing of all beings will anchor.

————————— Invocation —————————

Angels, please help me see future timelines with detachment, clarity and integrity, and trust that I will be shown them in divine perfect timing.

Guiding Angels:
Archangel Haniel, Archangel Metatron, Archangel Ariel

DAY 186

Channelled Angel message

We can help you with any situation you are finding challenging.

There is always guidance available to assist you, and we are always with you.

Solutions come in many forms.

If you are finding a situation difficult, we first remind you to ask for our assistance. We respect your free will. When you ask, we will respond. Always.

When you ask for assistance, we invite you to let go of what form this assistance will look like. The guidance or solution that we bring you will be the highest priority for you right now. It will be the next step. It will offer the solution or message that you need most. It may not be what you think you need.

We invite you to practise speaking with us daily. This opens energetic pathways that create a 'remembering' of your Angelic connection. You know our language and how to speak with us on a soul level. Practice activates this recall.

We invite you to remember that every experience has divine perfection. Life is not meant to be perfect. Life is an exploration of miracles, and as such includes all aspects of experience. There is no better than or worse than. There is no easier pathway. There is no better life.

Your life is a miracle. Every experience is a miracle. Every moment is a miracle. Love is the reason for your life, and it exists in every moment, even in the painful ones.

You do not need to navigate this journey alone. Love is always available to you. Love is within you and all around you.

Practising speaking with us does not just open you to our guidance and support; it opens your heart chakra to universal creation consciousness. Love becomes who you are. Your heart feels peaceful and accepting during the challenges.

There is always a pathway. It is love. And we are here to assist you as you find the way.

―――――――― Invocation ――――――――

Angels, please help me see, hear, and feel your loving guidance easily. Please remind me to ask for assistance, and to let go of the outcome.

Guiding Angels:
Guardian Angels, Archangel Faith, Archangel Raziel

DAY 187

Channelled Angel message

Learning to trust in the divine is part of the awakening process. Your heart is your guide.

You are not separate from the divine. You are an expression of it. You are the divine.

You are God. You are universal consciousness. You are love.

You are creation.

As you experience your awakening, this seed of understanding begins to grow and blossom within your heart.

Your heart guides you through your awakening as you remember a feeling, a knowing that you are eternal, that you are one with all living beings, that you are we.

Your heart is your energetic connection to this process. Your heart guides you with emotions and feelings that trigger your stages of remembering and awakening.

Trust and faith are a fundamental part of this process.

As you awaken, you find yourself questioning the validity of logic versus intuition.

Of thinking versus feeling.

Your feeling centre is your most underused and most powerful gift.

Your heart is the gateway to your intuition, to your ability to heal, to your ability to love, and to your ability to create miracles.

Your heart awakening is part of a collective heart awakening.

Miracles that you cannot conceive of await.

Love is the way, your heart knows the language, and you are safe to trust your heart.

—————— Invocation ——————

Angels, please help me open my heart now and awaken to the infinite love of the divine.

Guiding Angels:
Archangel Haniel, Archangel Chamuel, Archangel Uriel

DAY 188

Channelled Angel message

You are safe to witness and heal your shadow now.

As you witness your darkness, you also witness the collective darkness. They are connected as all are one.

As you allow yourself to see trauma, you also heal it.

Trauma is being revealed now. For one and for the collective.

Darkness is only that which is hidden.

It is here to be healed and brought to the light.

This happens first by acknowledging that which is hidden.

The collective shadow healing will occur as you acknowledge and heal your own shadow—that which is hidden, unhealed or unacknowledged in you.

Please seek assistance on your shadow-healing journey—from us, but also from your human support team of qualified sacred guides, healers, and professionals.

If your purpose is to bring light to the world and reveal the shadow, then we also ask that you continue to do your own shadow work now, and to be compassionate with yourself on this journey as your own deepest shadows are exposed.

Layers are being revealed at a fast rate for you and for all.

The light is here to support you. This is the purpose of the shift, of the great awakening.

To reveal that which has been hidden.

Your capacity to serve is directly proportionate to your healing.

———————— Invocation ————————

Angels, please assist me through my own shadow-healing journey as I integrate my wounds, trauma, and veils so that I may experience healing and enlightenment.

DAY 189

Channelled Angel message

New Earth is birthed via compassion and love.

As you navigate your own ascension process, we wish to assist you.

The shift occurring now has not occurred before at any time in human history.

There is no roadmap or blueprint from previous human memory in physical or light form.

The roadmap is one that exists in your heart.

It is one that you recall with a knowing that you can't explain. It is one that you recall from a remembering of a future vision. It is one that you feel within your energy and heart.

New Earth is created by actions that are rebellious, loving, and heart guided.

New Earth is created by actions that fly in the face of the current earth experience.

New Earth is created through embodiment of all that you wish to see in the world.

New Earth requires kindness, forgiveness, compassion, peace, and love as its blueprint.

New Earth is birthed within your own consciousness.

——————— Invocation ———————

Angels, please help me embody the vision of New Earth as I see it and feel it in my own mind/body/spirit.

Guiding Angels:
Archangel Faith, Archangel Metatron, Archangel Michael

DAY 190

Channelled Angel message

You are powerful beyond belief. A miracle.

Have you forgotten your radiance?

Miracles exist all around you. And you are indeed a miracle.

You are deeply loving, creative, kind, joyous, capable, and loveable.

Every part of you is worthy of expression.

Every part of you is needed now.

You are not meant to be like another, to conform, or to shrink to fit in.

You are meant to be you.

You know your truth and no other has the right to take ownership of your beliefs, body, ideas, or feelings.

You are here for a reason, and that is to love, be loved and be you in all your full glory.

You are awakening now to the remembering of your magnificence, and your sovereignty.

This is a journey of love, and it is a journey of loving yourself. As you love yourself, you love all others. For all are one.

Now is the time of discovery, awakening and remembering.

Your imagination and dreams are both the gateway and pathway through this shift.

That which can be imagined can be.

You are divine perfection in this moment and always.

Angels, please help me feel safe expressing all aspects of myself without limitations or fear.

Guiding Angels:
Archangel Michael, Archangel Nathaniel, Archangel Haniel

DAY 191

Channelled Angel message

Manifestation and creation operate on a divine timeframe. What you desire is forming now. Enjoy the process.

This process is energetic.

You are shifting your vibration to be a match to that which you desire.

The process is the purpose and reason for being. Life is the process of expansion of frequency and consciousness.

The process you are in now is of expansion to a new frequency level.

This is making you aware of that which is no longer in alignment as well as that which you desire.

The journey between identifying your desire and its manifestation in form can feel uncomfortable, but only when you are attached and resisting the journey.

We remind you that this process is also miraculous.

There are gifts in every stage, and you can allow yourself to notice and enjoy these moments along the way.

Your world distracts you with messages that you are less than if you do not have that which you desire, and that you should find it instantly.

We wish to guide you to find peace in the moment, and to

allow the process to be slow.

Slow is powerful. Allowing is powerful. It is acceptance of the divine perfection in the timing of all things.

All things happen with perfect timing. It is your acceptance of this that shifts your experience of the journey.

—————— Invocation ——————

Angels, please help me let go and flow with the experience I am having now, and trust that all is in perfect divine timing.

Guiding Angels:
Archangel Ariel, Archangel Faith, Archangel Grace

DAY 192

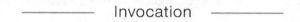

Miracles occur when you realise a new perspective.

Your energy is vast.

Your capabilities are infinite.

Your worth is innate

Your ability to heal, grow, and experience miracles is limitless.

You are an expression of God.

As you heal, distortions are recognised and released from your belief system, energy body and physical body.

Your aura heals and expands with every shift and integration.

You become your full potential with each shift and integration.

You experience awareness shifts and see through the distortions to new pathways with each healing.

You are the miracle.

Full, loving expression of self is the pathway.

Angels, please help me remember that I am worthy, capable and one with the divine now as I navigate my healing and ascension journey.

Guiding Angels:
Archangel Jophiel, Archangel Uriel, Archangel Metatron

DAY 193

Channelled Angel message

Pay attention to fear broadcasts and energetic distortions distracting you from your power.

There is a tremendous acceleration of the shift in consciousness now.

Your awareness is expanding and contracting in waves that gradually spiral outwards.

Each time you practise love and compassion for self and others, each time you practise forgiveness of self and others, you heal and become more whole.

The contractions occur when you are experiencing fear, pain, trauma or hurt.

We invite you to become curious about these lower frequencies.

Does this energy belong to you? Is this your emotional body indicating a healing opportunity?

Or is this energy outside of yourself, something that you are responding to with your strong empathic and intuitive abilities? In this case, we invite you to practise discernment, curiosity, investigation, and then energetic cleansing to let go and release this energetic distortion or fear projection.

If it does not belong to you, do not let it reside in your mind, body, or spirit.

Practise compassion for self and all beings, and let it go with love.

The great awakening will show you how much has been hidden, both within and in your awareness of the collective.

Remember that you do not need to enmesh with the collective energy and remember that the collective energy is filled with an intentional fear broadcast now.

Practise strong boundaries and hold your own light in radiant expansion.

———————— Invocation ————————

Angels, please help me identify any and all fear broadcasts or energy distortions in my field and awareness. Please help me have strong energetic boundaries and release all that is not mine with compassion and ease.

Guiding Angels: Archangel Michael

DAY 194

Channelled Angel message

Darkness and light are vibrations.

Darkness and light are energy frequencies.

Darkness is that which is unseen, unhealed, inverted, and fearful. It is that which harms self and other. Darkness as a vibration is contracted.

Light is that which is seen, accepted, forgiven, and healed. It is loving to self and other. Light as a vibration is expansive.

Darkness can be witnessed and healed with love and transmuted to light.

This process is fundamental to your human experience now.

Witnessing your own darkness, your shadow, your unhealed aspects of self, your trauma and your pain is what brings you the expansion, healing, and miracles you desire.

On an energetic level, each time you heal a shadow aspect of yourself, you expand and raise your frequency.

Darkness is not bad. It is an experience.

Darkness is not something that needs to be avoided. That is like saying you are to be avoided, healing is to be avoided, love is to be avoided.

Darkness is rising to be witnessed and healed on an individual and collective level now. It is the catalyst to ascension and enlightenment.

Darkness and light exist in varying degrees in every human incarnate now.

As you witness and heal your own shadow, you raise your frequency. This has a direct impact on the collective frequency.

The most powerful thing you can do to help the many is to heal yourself, identify where you are unloving to yourself and others, practise loving compassion, and heal.

You do not need to fear darkness. Quite the opposite. It is your most powerful guide.

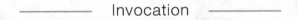

Invocation

Angels, please help me feel safe exploring and seeing my own shadows, veils and darkness, so that I can heal and raise my vibration.

Guiding Angels:
Archangel Raphael, Archangel Zadkiel, Archangel Metatron

DAY 195

Channelled Angel message

Twin-flame consciousness is activating now.

Twin-flame energy is not yet embodied on Earth.

It is a 5D frequency of universal consciousness expressed as union.

Twin-flame consciousness is being activated in both men and women who hold a blueprint of helping anchor this frequency for the collective now.

Twin-flame union is a spiritual union that will be explored in physical union.

The full embodiment of twin-flame union currently exists only in the fifth and sixth densities.

The message of twin-flame union has been distorted to create a desire for a perfect union, and feelings of less than, or unworthiness, for those who question why they have not achieved twin-flame union.

Twin-flame union is a journey by the one.

As you focus on love, self-love, love for others and love for all, your vibration becomes that of love. You are then able to explore twin-flame union within your own perception, and then with another.

This exploration and anchoring of twin-flame consciousness requires shadow work and light work.

This exploration is of the imperfect and unhealed.

This exploration is the next wave of healing the divine masculine and divine feminine through relationship.

Twin-flame consciousness is birthed through the fire of healing.

Twin-flame consciousness is fluid and moving, as the flames of two beings interact to explore union and separation.

Twin-flame union heals the multi-generational trauma and wounds of karma as the individual explores their own shadow through relationship with another.

This is also a soulmate relationship, with the specific theme of anchoring a healed aspect of divine union.

The exploration of twin-flame consciousness will activate healing for the collective with respect to all that is unhealed in the areas of sexual trauma, sexual violence, sexual shame, and all that has created separation between the divine masculine and divine feminine.

This process has begun.

When you see the shadow in the collective, know that this is the light bringing a new pathway to twin-flame union.

———— Invocation ————

Angels, please help me release all attachments to a perfect twin-flame relationship, so that I may open to experience the relationship and love presenting for me right now in this moment.

Guiding Angels:
Archangel Chamuel, Archangel Zadkiel, Archangel Nathaniel

DAY 196

Channelled Angel message

What you seek already exists. You need not seek it. It flows to you as you allow it in divine perfect timing.

The journey from here to there is sacred.

You are becoming what you seek.

Every moment on this journey is a miracle worth honouring and exploring.

Every step is part of the creation and blossoming.

You need not push, force, or control this experience.

This is faith, surrender, appreciation, joy and calm.

This is flow, intuition, observation, learning and understanding.

This is discovery of self, exploration of self, curiosity, and intrigue.

This is passion, authenticity, vulnerability, and radiance.

Do you see now why you cannot force this experience?

For you would miss the most wonderful parts.

———— Invocation ————

Angels, please help me let go and trust that all is occurring in divine perfect order to bring me that which I desire at the exact right time.

Guiding Angels: Archangel Faith, Archangel Ariel

DAY 197

Channelled Angel message

Compassion and acceptance will dissolve all separation.

Everything is a perception.

Your perception of another as other, as different, as wrong, as to blame, as the reason for your pain, or as the problem, creates a division and separation.

As you awaken, we invite you to remember that there is only one. You are one with all beings.

All experiences are valid. Why would they not be? They are valid because they exist.

All experiences have a reason, and there is divine perfection in every experience, even the ones you deem as painful.

All feelings are valid, yours and all others.

All knowledge is valid.

All opinions are valid.

Where do you hold beliefs that create judgement, pain, or separation?

This is your direct pathway through this challenge.

Your feelings are the guide and the path to healing.

How can you love? How can you connect with this person who is a mirror to your perception? For that is the way through your experience.

Love, acceptance, and compassion are the pathway to healing and to unity.

Love, acceptance, and compassion are the pathway to the miracles you seek.

Seek first within yourself, and you will find it in another.

Your own perception is the only one you can heal. For you are the only one that exists. Just as you are also the other, and all are one.

———— Invocation ————

Angels, as I experience pain from another, please help me turn within to find compassion and acceptance and begin healing my own shadows and wounds.

Guiding Angels:
Archangel Zadkiel, Archangel Raguel, Archangel Michael

DAY 198

Channelled Angel message

That which you desire exists. Your job is to move from here to there.

As you begin to feel, imagine and dream of that which you

desire, we want to explain that this is your intuition speaking with you.

You are having an energetic response to that which already exists.

Your now frequency is interacting with your future-self frequency and showing you the vibrational shift required to align at the same place.

Your journey is to align your frequency with that which you feel within your energy field, that which you desire, that which you dream of.

This process is one of faith, allowing, healing and love.

Love for self is the key.

Love for self-activates every step of your frequency shift.

You cannot force this process. Can you force a flower to bloom?

You are blooming at your divine perfect pace, and the journey is a miracle.

Trust and faith in yourself require resilience and strength that you have not been taught.

We wish to assist you to remember that you are a powerful, miraculous being of love.

You are becoming that which you seek.

Blossom now.

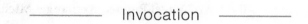

Invocation

Angels, please remind me that as I identify that which I desire, it has already occurred, so I can let go and blossom into becoming one with the frequency of my desire.

Guiding Angels:
Archangel Ariel, Archangel Jophiel, Archangel Faith

DAY 199

Channelled Angel message

The task is to become what you seek.

What you seek already exists, as frequency.

As you begin to seek it, you are in fact noticing this vibration, and interacting with it energetically.

That which you seek is an aspect of yourself.

That which you seek is a mirror or aspect of what exists already.

That which you seek is a message that you indeed are worthy, can create this, and will, as it is already in existence. It is you speaking with you.

That which you seek is that which you are!

The journey is that which is already laid out before you, that you cannot see.

The journey is the discovery of the pathway, the healing, the ideas, the actions, the awareness, the growth, the integration.

The journey is but a shift.

The shift is both minuscule and infinite.

Your awareness of what you desire should be celebrated as a whisper of that which you are becoming and that which you already are!

————— Invocation —————

Angels, please help me let go and flow with the journey of becoming who I am in divine timing.

Guiding Angels:
Archangel Faith, Archangel Nathaniel, Archangel Ariel

DAY 200

Channelled Angel message

You become that which you desire by loving yourself.

Love is the pathway to all healing, and all creation.

Love is the miracle energy that makes that which you desire come to form.

As you imagine and love, you create.

All that you imagine can be created.

All that you desire exists.

You are the creation force. You are the creator. You are God expressed as form.

You are infinitely powerful and infinitely loving. This combination makes you human.

Your capacity to love directly correlates to your capacity to create.

Your desires are only limited by your capacity to love, which is infinite. Do you see?

This is a remembering. An awakening.

Once you recall your full capacity to love, all that you can imagine and all that you desire will birth through you, both individually and collectively.

New Earth is birthing via a collective remembering, a collective awakening to love.

To support this process, all you need to do is love, dream, imagine, heal, and create.

Loving yourself is healing yourself.

You change the world now via your commitment to heal yourself and to love yourself.

We invite you to focus on love. Envelop yourself in love. Surround yourself in love. Explore love. Be curious about love. Be compassionate and forgiving about love. Embody love.

Angels, in every moment that I find painful or challenging,
please show me the pathway of love.

Guiding Angels:
Archangel Chamuel, Archangel Faith, Archangel Haniel

DAY 201

Channelled Angel message

Your heart is your power centre.

Everything that you desire will flow to you in direct proportion to the capacity that you give and receive love.

As you open your heart, you heal.

As you love yourself, you heal.

As you love freely, your intuition blossoms.

As you love, you become a channel for the divine.

As you love, you connect more deeply with all beings.

The more you focus on love and opening your sensitive, beautiful heart, the more you experience the life you desire.

Love is your gift. Love is what created you and every other consciousness.

Love is what makes you human.

It is not unsafe to love. It is the very power that you hold to transform your life.

When you shut off love, you shut off the power to create, to manifest, to connect, to receive and to heal—and, indeed, you shut off your humanity.

Open your heart. Love freely. It is the gateway to the miracles you desire.

Angels, please help me begin to gently open my heart now so that I may become a channel and vessel for the expression of infinite love.

Guiding Angels:
Archangel Chamuel, Archangel Raphael, Archangel Uriel

DAY 202

Channelled Angel message

When you lose your sense of connection to the light, go to nature.

You are an energetic being, and you require regular physical contact with Gaia in order to have optimum vitality and wellness.

Your being is designed to be in energetic connection with Mother Gaia—in vibrational harmony and in frequency alignment.

When you feel out of sync, when you lose hope, when you feel despairing, sad, afraid, or confused, go to nature.

Your power, clarity and energy are healed and restored in nature.

Your intuition is stronger in nature.

You will hear our messages and feel our loving presence more easily in nature.

You will experience energetic realignment and attunement when in nature.

You will heal in nature.

Gaia has a frequency that is here to unconditionally support your physical experience on Earth. You are supported in every way by Gaia! All your physical and energetic needs are met with vast love by Gaia.

In order to fully receive this loving gift of energy, you need to be in physical contact with Gaia daily.

The more light you need, the more healing you require, the more time you will need to spend in nature.

You will become re-calibrated to the frequency of Mother Gaia and to the light in nature.

Light is the energy of love and the creation force.

Nature is your energetic battery. The conductor of light. The conductor of love.

How can you adjust your days to allow yourself more time in nature?

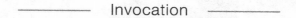 Invocation

Angels, please give me daily reminders to spend more time in nature, especially when I feel disconnected, sad, or despairing, so that I can clear and restore my energy and reconnect with the infinite love of the divine.

Guiding Angels:
Archangel Gersisa, Archangel Ariel, Archangel Raphael

DAY 203

Channelled Angel message

The journey of another is not your concern.

Their behaviour, actions, choices, opinions, and feelings belong to them.

Your behaviour, actions, choice, opinions, and feelings belong to you.

Your task is to practise loving acceptance, compassion, and kindness towards all others, and to yourself.

It is not your job to awaken another. Awakening is a sacred journey that will activate within each soul at its divine perfect moment, or not. For some may choose not to awaken in this lifetime.

By presuming authority over the awakening, journey, or pathway of another, you violate their free will and sovereignty.

But when the world sleeps, and the truth calls to you, how can you serve the light, you ask?

Your pathway is within.

Your pathway is service.

First, find the light within yourself.

Then, serve others as they find the light within themselves.

This has always been the pathway.

Your pathway to service exists already.

You find it by finding the light within yourself.

Invocation

Angels, please remind me to practise unconditional acceptance and compassion for the choices of all beings, even and especially when I don't understand or agree with them.

Guiding Angels:
Archangel Zadkiel, Archangel Michael, Archangel Grace

DAY 204

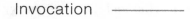
Channelled Angel message

We have always been with you.

The love that we hold for you is infinite.

We see you in all your radiance, all your vast light, all your humanity and so-called imperfections.

We see you as magnificent, an aspect of God, and capable of miraculous, wondrous experiences.

You have the power to create. To love. To learn. To grieve.

You have the power to expand your consciousness, to heal yourself and others, to be a conduit for the expression of the divine.

Your heart, your capacity to love, is what makes you human, and miraculous.

Your ability to love is what connects you to all living beings, to us, and to God.

Your ability to love is the pathway to feeling our presence and hearing our messages.

Your ability to love is the pathway to all the change that you desire.

Your ability to love is the pathway to life.

We whisper to you with the language of love. To unlock our messages, we ask you to unlock your heart.

You are meant to feel. How can you love if your heart is locked away?

You are safe to open your heart and we cannot wait to speak with you!

――――――― Invocation ―――――――

Angels, please assist me on the next step of opening and healing my heart now.

Guiding Angels:
Archangel Zadkiel, Archangel Chamuel, Archangel Raphael

DAY 205

Channelled Angel message

Fear is the gateway to healing.

Fear is a spiritual lesson, fear is temporary.

Fear is a message. Fear is your higher-self whispering to you, showing you the pathway.

Fear is something that is here to show you the way forwards. Fear is a messenger and a guide.

When you experience fear, we invite you to become curious.

What am I afraid of?

Is this fear true?

How can I learn more about this situation?

Is the thing I am afraid of something that exists, or something that I am remembering from the past, or imagining may occur in the future?

Is this likely? Is it just as likely that something else may occur, or better still, is it more likely that something far better and far more amazing will occur?

How can I become curious and sovereign and trusting of my own intuition in the experience of fear?

How can I reclaim my energetic power and walk myself through fear responses?

How can I find love and feel my heart when I feel fear?

Your heart is the pathway through fear; your heart and your capacity to love are the pathway to healing.

Everything is here to help you heal, and fear is the first step on that pathway.

———— Invocation ————

Angels, please help me walk through my fear to discover the healing, miracles and lessons that await me on the other side.

DAY 206

Channelled Angel message

Despair is atomised with joy, love, music, nature, and laughter.

Despair is an energy that can be shifted and alchemised.

Despair, like many shadow emotions, is part of the human experience.

When you identify the feelings of despair or hopelessness, you may feel that your connection to source has been severed. We remind you that you are always connected to the divine.

Despair, hopelessness, and all other shadow emotions are not a permanent state. They are but a steppingstone to a higher state of awareness. You can shift your energy once you find a place of complete acceptance with your shadow feelings.

Despair is currently being broadcast in the collective as an attempt to disconnect you from source and keep you in a state of fear, with the sole intention of shutting down the mass awakening.

You alchemise and neutralise despair with acceptance, grace, and love.

When you identify despair, hopelessness, and fear in the collective, be mindful of your sensitive energy and choose to switch off from the broadcast.

Clear your energy and your heart by immersing yourself in all that brings you joy.

Love, hug, dance, laugh and sing!

Sit with the birds and bees. Open your heart to the sky and to your loved ones and send compassion and acceptance to all humans.

To love is to feel. To connect to the divine is to open your heart.

Practise awareness of your energy and consciously connect to the light.

──────── Invocation ────────

Angels, please help me swiftly move through feelings of fear, despair, and hopelessness, and find unconditional acceptance for myself and all beings, so that I can return to the light with grace.

Guiding Angels:
Archangel Michael, Archangel Grace, Archangel Chamuel

DAY 207

Channelled Angel message

You have everything you need.

You are divine perfection.

You are able to love, to learn, to create, to laugh, to heal, to manifest, and to create life.

You are literally the expression of God. A miracle.

You are radiant! You are so filled with love and light that we see you and we are in awe of your magnificence!

We have infinite love for you exactly as you are; there are no faults within you. Everything is exactly as it should be for your experience.

Your own experience is perfect too. It is perfect in its depth; the magic lies in the journey and the journey is beautiful in all its shades and shadows.

You are so powerful that you have no idea what you are truly capable of.

You need nothing! Everything you require exists when you are ready to realise and harness it.

You become ready at the exact right moment. You need

not push this journey of life, this journey of expansion of consciousness, this journey of love.

There is nothing that is controlling you. You are free!

There is nothing that will change your experience, other than your own shift in perception.

There is nothing stopping you from creating a thing that you desire, other than your own consciousness.

You are the miracle. You are the creator. You are the lover. You are the one. You are what you seek, and the pathway is within.

—————— Invocation ——————

Angels, please remind me that I am the creator, and that as I imagine and love, I create miracles.

Guiding Angels: Archangel Uriel, Archangel Faith

DAY 208

Every experience has meaning.

Your human journey is a wondrous miracle.

Every moment is filled with opportunities for love.

Love exists in every moment.

Love exists in challenges, in pain, in suffering and in death, as well as in joy, in success, in overcoming and in birth.

Love is full spectrum.

You are consciousness expressed as love, in form.

You are radiant and eternal.

Your limits only exist when you create them.

Every single experience you have is in divine perfect order.

There is never a mistake. Every choice, every thought, every feeling is an opportunity to express love and to learn about love.

Every moment activates you in divine perfection for the pathway you are travelling.

Every pause is exquisite in its ability to create space for the process to come together.

Every challenge perfectly creates opportunities for healing, learning, and understanding.

Every experience of suffering gives you an understanding of love expressed through pain, grief, loss or hardship.

There is no less-than experience. There is no better-than experience. When you return to the light, you will see them all equally and with wonder as part of the miracle.

You chose to participate in the full spectrum of the human experience, in all its wondrous depth and shade.

The experience is the miracle.

—————— Invocation ——————

Angels, please help me see all experiences equally, and become curious as to the miracle unfolding in this moment.

Guiding Angels: Archangel Jeremiel, Archangel Grace

DAY 209

Channelled Angel message

Your light impacts all those you come into contact with.

You are a radiant being of light!

When you expand into your radiance, you shine love in all directions around you. Your power to heal yourself and all those you interact with magnifies a thousandfold.

Light is love. Love is light.

As you reclaim and expand into your light, you help anchor light everywhere you go.

Love/light activates light.

Love/light cuts through all darkness.

Love/light heals all wounds.

Love/light exposes all shadows for healing.

It is your light that is your greatest power.

It is your love that is your greatest power.

Light is the way; love is the way. Love was always the way.

Being a lightworker is both an act of rebellion, and a practice.

Embodying love/light will require dedication and practice.

This is not a thinking journey, but a feeling journey.

All that you seek lies inwards via your heart, and as you activate your heart, light shines the way for all those around you.

If you wish to be of service to others and to the light now, you must first find the light within.

Seek love in yourself, heal yourself, and find your own light. This is the fastest way to serve the collective now.

Your radiant light is needed. Your journey to light is needed.

———————— Invocation ————————

Angels, please remind me that my capacity to serve others increases in direct proportion to the amount that I honour and love myself.

Guiding Angels:
Archangel Jophiel, Archangel Metatron, Archangel Michael

DAY 210

Channelled Angel message

Everything you desire comes as you raise your frequency. As you love.

You are an energetic being. That energy is that which you call love/light.

Love and light are the frequency of creation.

Your desires, hopes and dreams are a frequency reaction to that which exists in a future/now reality.

You are receiving an energetic transmission showing you the blueprint of the journey from here to there.

That which you call manifesting is an energetic experience of raising your frequency to be a match with that which you desire.

Your pathway or method is to raise your frequency to be a match with the feeling of your desire.

Raising your frequency is also that which you call ascension. It is the journey of realisation.

That which raises your frequency is everything you love, everything that brings you joy, everything that brings you integration of your shadow, everything that heals you, everything that brings you acceptance of self and others.

This is the pathway.

———— Invocation ————

Angels, please show me the next step to shift my frequency to be a match with that which I desire.

Guiding Angels:
Archangel Michael, Archangel Metatron, Archangel Jophiel

DAY 211

Channelled Angel message

Everything happens in divine perfect timing.

Your journey from where you are to where you wish to be is one of faith and trust.

Your journey is one of flow.

Your journey is one of presence, love, and openness.

Your journey is one of frequency, awareness, and energy shifts.

Your journey is not linear, and it is one that involves many miraculous steps, people, and experiences. All these are orchestrated perfectly to support your experience.

Your journey is exactly that which creates the outcome.

It is the journey, the presence, the now that is the focal point for you.

As you pull your energy back from that which you desire, into now and into presence, into being here now in this moment, you create that which you desire!

It is your 'now' experience and energy that creates your future.

You can let go now and see what is right here and now for you.

———————— Invocation ————————

Angels, as I identify the pathway to my future desires, please help me let go and trust that all is well in this moment, and that I am exactly where I am meant to be.

Guiding Angels:
Archangel Faith, Archangel Jeremiel, Archangel Ariel

DAY 212

Channelled Angel message

Faith is an act of surrender.

Remember, we are with you now and always.

When you let go and surrender to the divine, this can feel uncomfortable.

When you let go, this can sometimes trigger feelings of fear and a discomfort with the unfamiliar. A sense of being out of control.

This is what a leap of faith feels like.

This feeling is your heart opening to trust the divine.

You are not unsafe.

As you open your heart and let go, you are then able to feel our love and our unconditional acceptance more easily. You are able to feel that great love that is the energy of light, source, creation and God.

Letting go is the first step to remembering that you are indeed not alone.

Letting go is the ultimate act of rebellion, as you must first trust in your own heart, your own inner knowing and your own energy.

Your heart is your guidance system.

Your heart is that which connects you to us, to all beings and to God.

Opening your heart is the ultimate act of surrender.

You are not alone. You are loved and accepted infinitely by us and by the infinite love consciousness that is the source of all creation. God.

Let go now. You are safe to open your heart to the divine.

Angels, please help me let go of all resistance and open my heart to the infinite love of the divine. Please help me know that these feelings of fear will pass, and that I am safe to open my heart now.

Guiding Angels:
Archangel Michael, Archangel Uriel, Archangel Faith

DAY 213

Channelled Angel message

Every challenge can be worked through with love.

We understand that life can feel very difficult sometimes.

There is always a pathway through these challenges.

We see you struggle with feeling alone, and we remind you that you are truly never alone.

We love you in every moment. We are with you in every moment. We accept you exactly as you are, wholly and completely, in every moment.

Love is the pathway through all your challenges. Love creates opportunities for compassion, acceptance, forgiveness, connection, growth and understanding.

Resistance to love creates fear, heart walls, disconnection, anger, blame and hurt.

Life is an exploration of love.

Love is the pathway through your most difficult moments.

You are an infinitely loving being. Your capacity to love is what makes you human. It is your brilliance, your creativity, your inspiration, your intuition, your kindness, your compassion, and your acceptance.

Your love creates miracles of consciousness shifts. It repairs, heals, and connects.

You are safe to love.

────── Invocation ──────

Angels, when I feel most alone in my struggle, please show me the path of love. Please remind me that you are with me, that I am loved, that I am love.

Guiding Angels:
Archangel Chamuel, Archangel Michael, Archangel Uriel

DAY 214

Channelled Angel message

Your heart is the key to the transformation you seek.

Love is the healing force.

You are safe to open your heart.

You are safe to love.

You are safe to feel.

You are safe to use your intuition.

You are safe to hope, dream, have faith, and trust.

You are safe to express your feelings.

Every part of you is an expression of love waiting to be realised.

Opening your heart is the first step towards full expression of your authentic loving self.

Your potential is absolutely limitless!

What you desire, and much more, exists on the journey of heart healing and loving self and others.

Love is the energy and expression of miraculous divine creation. You are love in form.

Everything that you can conceive of is possible. You create it with the energy of love!

Your heart is the key.

Angels, I am ready to begin co-creating with the divine now.
Please help me open my heart to be a conduit for and receiver of
the infinite love of the divine.

Guiding Angels:
Archangel Ariel, Archangel Chamuel, Archangel Uriel

DAY 215

Channelled Angel message

Your heart is your barometer and guide.

We watch every experience you have, and love and accept you completely.

We support you unconditionally.

Our messages are here to activate, to validate and to empower.

We will not reveal the answers you seek, as this violates your free will and your purpose for being.

We will guide you with messages that assist you on your journey.

All that you seek exists within your own heart.

Your heart is a finely tuned instrument that communicates to you via the energetic language of love.

All that you seek can be found in self-enquiry and communication with your heart.

Your heart guides you every step of the way with powerful messages.

Every emotion or response to life's circumstances is a message from your heart to be decoded.

Understanding these messages is the key to the steps on your journey.

Having the support of a sacred guide can assist you to begin to learn the language of your own heart.

There are many who speak sacred heart language and can help you awaken to your innate knowledge of your own heart language.

Your heart awakening is safe.

You are safe to love. You are safe to receive love. You are safe to heal. Love is your healer.

Invocation

Angels, please help me find a sacred guide to assist me on the journey of opening my heart and learning my sacred heart language.

Guiding Angels:
Archangel Raphael, Archangel Zadkiel, Archangel Chamuel

DAY 216

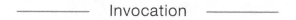
Channelled Angel message

Your vibration brings you your match.

We speak of energetic circuitry, of the wheel of possibility, of co-creation.

We speak of intention and your resonance with that which you desire.

Your heart is the centre of your energy field and radiates with the vibration of your consciousness.

You raise your vibration by healing and loving. By opening your heart and learning its language.

Love is your creation force, your magnet, and closing off to love slows this process.

Love is that which communicates with others as a vibrational language that all can learn to understand.

Love is that which attracts your desires, responds to matching frequency options, shows you the way via resonance, and creates the next wave of expansion.

Love helps you through challenges, heals you and transforms your awareness.

Everything you know about life until now has been from a thinking perspective.

As the individual and collective shift into 5D frequency and unity consciousness, love will become the language needed to both transform and create the new earth reality.

Learning to open your heart and understand and harness the messages and creation energy of your own loving vibration is your purpose.

A sacred heart guide can assist you to activate this process.

A sacred heart guide is a healer who you resonate with.

They come in many forms. Ask us to help you connect with your sacred guide.

─────── Invocation ───────

Angels, please help me find a sacred heart guide, and give me a clear sign that I feel as a resonance in my heart so that I might recognise them.

Guiding Angels:
Archangel Raphael, Archangel Zadkiel, Archangel Chamuel

DAY 217

Channelled Angel message

Fear creates division. Love is the pathway to unity.

When you feel afraid, your heart closes off to love and connection.

Fear has been intentionally inserted in the social consciousness to create division disguised as protection. *Do not let yourself be hurt. Protect yourself. Keep safe. They are other. You have much to fear.*

Everything that you seek is found in open-hearted loving, in connection.

The pathway to all that you desire is in all that is love.

Fear creates division. Division separates you from self, from others and from the infinite source of all love.

Love frequency is connective and healing.

Love frequency is consciousness shifting, for one and many.

Love frequency is that which you feel. Your emotions are expressions of love frequency, and all are safe to be felt and expressed.

Love frequency connects you to that which you saw as other, but which is also an aspect of yourself, for all are one.

Universal consciousness exists in both separated awareness and unity state.

The current collective shift is from fear to love.

The current collective shift is from division to unity.

The current individual shift is from fear to love.

The current individual shift is from division to unity.

The current collective shift is from separation to oneness.

Where is there fear in your life? Where is there division in relationship to self, other, or the source of all creation?

Love is the pathway to peaceful reconnection to self, source and other, and embodiment of unity consciousness.

We can assist you on this shift.

–––––––––– Invocation ––––––––––

Angels, please help me see through the veil of fear and find the pathway to love, unity and oneness.

Guiding Angels: Archangel Michael, Archangel Butyalil

DAY 218

Channelled Angel message

God/source is love consciousness.

That which you understand as God is a conscious expression of infinite love.

That which you understand as God is that which expresses love in form via conscious creation.

That which you understand as God is infinite love.

There is no religion in what you understand as God.

When you interact with God, there is only infinite love.

The rules of God are not as you understand them.

The rules are in fact not rules but expressions of creation in balanced unity.

And so, there is only love, and resistance to love.

All experience stems from expression of love or resistance to love.

And so, we ask you to know that God, or love consciousness, is both expansive and infinite and accepting entirely of any resistance to love.

This is the polarity of the human experience.

In order to experience life, both are present.

You came here to co-create and explore love.

All that you experience is an awareness of love/resistance to love.

All that you desire comes from understanding and working with love and resistance to love.

This is the only law.

──────── Invocation ────────

Angels, please remind me that my only purpose is to experience love, as an expression of the one infinite creator.

Guiding Angels: Archangel Uriel, Archangel Chamuel

DAY 219

Channelled Angel message

The current experience is in alignment with every living being.

There is a reason for every single experience.

Each experience is here to teach you and all others about love (and resistance to love).

There are agreements between you and all those you interact with to facilitate this experience.

This extends to every single being, and every single moment.

The experience is the reason for being.

The experience is perfect in that it allows for full exploration of all that is love via exploration of all that is resistance to love.

There is no bad experience. There is only experience.

The result is not the purpose. The experience is.

All who are here now chose this time to have this experience.

All who are here now chose the current lessons.

All who are here now are actively engaging in the collective consciousness process.

This is divine perfection expressed.

Every single event, every single breath, every single person, every single moment is divine perfection because it is.

This is the infinite expression of love.

This is the expression of creation.

This is indeed that which you understand as a miracle.

There is perfection in the fluid energetic interaction of all beings.

This is both destined and random at once.

It is destined because it occurs, and it is random because every being has free will.

And so, we ask you to open to the divine perfection of your own experience.

Everything is in perfect random order to present you with exactly the experience you need.

--------- Invocation ---------

Angels, please help me see my current experience as completely perfect in this moment, so that I can find the pathway to miracles.

Guiding Angels:
Archangel Jeremiel, Archangel Faith, Archangel Grace

DAY 220

Channelled Angel message

The experience of love is full spectrum.

You chose to come here for the experience of love and resistance to love.

As you experience resistance to love in all its forms, so you are able to find the presence of love.

For one does not exist without the other and both exist at once.

Love, and therefore life, is your awareness and expression of love.

There is no bad experience.

There is no good experience.

All experiences have a reason and the moment you accept them all as equal, you will find peace.

The spectrum of life and of love is a vibrational expression of movement.

It is dynamic and has opposing forces.

You are able to move with love as a dance.

—————— Invocation ——————

Angels, please help me find acceptance with all of life's experiences, so that I may find peace and love in any given moment.

Guiding Angels: Archangel Chamuel

DAY 221

Channelled Angel message

What you seek is seeking you. You are already connected.

As soon as you imagine that which you seek, that which you seek also imagines you.

The energy of love is that which creates. As you imagine what you desire, as you feel your love for what you desire, you connect with what exists already.

Your imagination is the key to your ability to create.

Your heart is the key to your imagination.

You are love. You create with love.

So, as you begin now to imagine that which you seek, you also create it; you feel it into existence, and that existence is now (as there is only now).

So, feel and imagine. And as you do, that which you seek feels and imagines you. For such is the power of the ripple of the quantum field.

--------- Invocation ---------

Angels, please remind me that there is only now, and that every thought, feeling, and desire is creating my reality in this moment.

Guiding Angels: Archangel Ariel, Archangel Grace

DAY 222

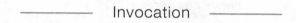

Channelled Angel message

As you let go, you allow all that you desire to appear.

There is truly no need to force or control your creation process.

Creation is love. It is magic, faith and flow.

Creation is a heart process of imagining that which you desire into existence.

Creation is also that which you call manifesting.

As you allow your heart to open, expand and radiate the full light of your magnificence, you become the vibration of your desire.

For your desire is in frequency alignment and circuitry with you.

It exists as soon as you imagine it.

The timing of its realisation is divine.

Allowing is a feminine energy.

The feminine exists within one and the collective, as all are one.

That which you desire exists already, and as you feel this truth with all your heart, you begin the process of magnifying it to you.

———————— Invocation ————————

Angels, please remind me that my vibration is that which creates, manifests, and draws my desires to me.

Guiding Angels:
Archangel Ariel, Archangel Jophiel, Archangel Metatron

DAY 223

Channelled Angel message

You can consciously shift your frequency and change your experience.

You are an expression of consciousness as love.

You are a physical, mental, and energetic expression.

You create your experience from a place of curiosity and willingness to explore all that is love.

As you become conscious, you begin to change your experience.

Perhaps you call this manifesting. Perhaps you call it healing. Perhaps you call it detachment. Perhaps you call it gratitude. Perhaps you call it love.

Love is a frequency, a feeling, an energy.

Love is a power that creates all living beings. The link between science, creation, consciousness, and love is unrealised.

Your frequency (which is your feelings, your thoughts, and your capacity to love) is something you can intentionally steer and change in any given moment.

As you change your frequency, you change your experience.

As you decide to raise your frequency over time, you begin the path of creation, of realisation and of ascension.

———————— Invocation ————————

Angels, please remind me that I can change my experience in any given moment by changing my frequency.

Guiding Angels: Archangel Metatron, Archangel Ariel

DAY 224

Channelled Angel message

Notice when you feel afraid or attached. This is a message from the divine.

You are an energetic being, and your frequency is a language you can learn to decipher and use as your guide.

Your emotions and feelings are signals and messages that guide you through your experience.

When you experience fear or feel attached to a situation, this is a message from the divine asking you to reconnect with the constant love of source.

All humans have access to the loving guidance of the Angels and of source/God.

This love and guidance is a frequency.

It is a feeling.

When you experience resistance to love, you can use this as a message to reconnect with love.

Attachment is an expression of fear. It is a form of control that contracts your energy field and prevents you from receiving the infinite abundance of the quantum field.

When you notice you are attached to a belief, situation, person or outcome, we invite you to notice that you are in fact preventing the outcome you desire from flowing to you.

There is a divine order to all things, a dynamic cause and effect.

That which you desire will come to you peacefully and spontaneously at the exact right time, and this process is aided by your willingness to be open and flow.

This is trust in the divine.

This is faith.

It requires your constant interaction, attention, and surrender.

It is a practice and is dynamic. Faith is a moving energy that you will dance with as life presents opportunities to explore love and resistance to love.

We remind you of your power to be a conscious participant.

———— Invocation ————

Angels, please remind me that fear and attachment contract my energy field and slow my creation process.

Guiding Angels:
Archangel Michael, Archangel Ariel, Archangel Metatron

DAY 225

Channelled Angel message

Everything is about love and resistance to love.

Every single experience is an expression of love or resistance to love.

This is the miracle of the human experience. Love does not

exist without understanding where you are resisting love.

Joy does not have meaning without sorrow.

Fear does not exist without trust.

The reason for existence is to express and experience love.

You are love expressed as form.

You are loving consciousness.

You are connected to all living things, and all are also an expression of the one consciousness. God is love, you are love, and so you are also God.

Love is the way you understand every experience.

Love is the solution to every challenge or problem.

In exploration of your experience, you will find the pathway before you as you look for love and observe where you are resisting love.

You are a co-creator and have the power of love at your fingertips at every given moment.

Life is a miraculous exploration of love, and we love you infinitely.

Finding love is by focusing on that which brings you love.

What do you love? Who do you love? Start there.

———————— Invocation ————————

Angels, please show me the love that exists right now in this moment.

Guiding Angels: Archangel Chamuel

DAY 226

Channelled Angel message

As you open your heart, you change your experience.

Your heart is that which connects you to all living beings, and to the divine.

Your heart transmits and receives love as a frequency.

That frequency is that which creates miracles. It created you. It is light, and it is love. You are light, you are love.

The love that you are able to give and receive is an energy that transmits via your heart.

Wounds, pain, and trauma can close your heart.

Compassion, acceptance, and forgiveness will open your heart.

As you open your heart, you increase your capacity to feel.

As you open your heart, you increase your capacity to love.

As you open your heart, you increase your capacity to receive.

As you open your heart, you restore the energetic light connection between you and all living beings and God, of which you are an expression.

As you reconnect with the divine, your intuition increases.

As you begin to both give and receive love, or transmit love, you expand your consciousness and begin to interact on a vibrational level with all living beings.

This is both your purpose and the pathway to find your purpose.

——————— Invocation ———————

Angels, please remind me that my highest priority is to open to give and receive love in any given moment.

Guiding Angels: Archangel Chamuel

DAY 227

Channelled Angel message

As you realise that you are divine radiant love, so too you realise all that you desire.

For the magic of creation lies within your own heart, and your heart is the magnet and the transmitter.

As you recall the truth of your full magnificence and expand slowly inwards into the full depths of your heart, you experience realisation.

All that you desire lies within.

All that you seek lies within.

You are love in full spectrum. Acceptance of your balanced expression of dark and light aspects of self and of love is the moment of realisation: you hold the creative power of love within your own hands.

And so, as you experience this within, you experience shifts in your external reality.

And so, as you expand into realisation that you are the love that you seek, the love that you are becomes realised in form.

Love attracts love.

Love creates love.

Be the love that you wish to receive in all areas of your life. You hold the power of transformation and creation in your hands.

————— Invocation —————

Angels, please remind me that only love exists, and that love is the answer in every moment. Please show me the path to love now.

Guiding Angels: Archangel Chamuel

DAY 228

Channelled Angel message

We speak a language that you remember and feel. Love.

Learning to speak with us is something everyone can do.

We know you. We knew you before you came into this physical experience.

We love you. We love and accept everything about you.

We will never judge you, shame you, be busy, speak down to you, turn away from you or abandon you.

We are here to assist you through every moment of your experience.

We are never far away, and we listen the moment you ask for assistance.

We speak the language of love, and we speak via the miracles of synchronicity and coincidence.

You can remember and learn to decode our messages.

All it takes is practice and faith.

With time, you can learn to hear our direct messages.

This is a feeling/knowing/memory experience.

We respect your free will. We do not predict the future nor violate the free will of another.

We can assist you with seeing the next step, and with clarity on that which you already know.

We send you love in waves. This is our most powerful and important role.

We remind you of your magnificence and we assist you to remember your power. You have the answers. You are divinely perfect. All is well. There is no reason to fear. You are love. You are the creator.

Angels, please remind me that there is no barrier, block, or limit to my ability to speak with you and receive your loving guidance.

Guiding Angels: Guardian Angels

DAY 229

Channelled Angel message

All you need to do is focus within. In every situation, you are the answer.

The answer you seek does not lie outside of yourself.

Your happiness is not dependent on another.

Your peace is not dependent on a situation changing.

Your worth is not in question, other than when you question it.

You being loveable is not determined by anyone other than yourself.

There is no change required outside of yourself that will shift your experience.

Your experience will shift when you shift.

Your awareness is the gateway to the experience you desire.

Your feelings are the energetic messages that guide you forwards to expand your consciousness.

As you decode your experience, you will also begin to shift your frequency, via love, acceptance, and forgiveness.

In any given challenge, we ask you to look within and start there.

You need not travel this journey alone. We will assist you. You can also call in a sacred guide to assist you in physical form when needed.

Angels, please remind me that all the answers I seek will be found within. Please help me find a sacred guide to assist me on my journey.

Guiding Angels: Guardian Angels

DAY 230

Channelled Angel message

Love is the energy of creation. Love is magic. You are the magician.

Love is the answer to everything.

Love is that which creates.

Love is the energy of manifesting.

Creation is imagining something into existence via your heart.

Your imagination is your most powerful creative tool, and your heart is the quantum 3D printer.

As you let go of all the external forces that seek to disconnect you from your heart and control your imagination via programming, you begin to realise that you are indeed a radiant, powerful being!

Love is both creation and destruction.

Love dissolves all fear.

The dissolution of the veil comes via the realisation of love.

You can apply this metaphor to any area where you see something created from fear. It can be dissolved with love.

Love knows no barriers.

Love creates miracles.

Love requires faith, resilience, trust, and courage.

You know the language of love. It is innate.

Your heart will always guide you.

Angels, please remind me that love dissolves all veils of fear both within and without.

Guiding Angels:
Archangel Chamuel, Archangel Michael, Archangel Faith

DAY 231

Channelled Angel message

Sacred guides come in all forms.

They are friends, strangers, therapists, healers, mentors, and teachers.

When you feel ready to expand your journey, your sacred guide will appear.

They have a soul contract to work with you, one that was agreed upon prior to incarnation.

Sometimes it is one powerful conversation that activates an awareness shift. This is a sacred guide.

Sometimes it is a professional relationship over many years. This is a sacred guide.

Sometimes you have more than one sacred guide.

Sometimes you outgrow one guide, and another appears.

Sacred guides empower you and hold a light on the pathway that already exists before you.

Sacred guides do not act as a guru or require devotion. They know that you are your teacher and healer, and help you remember this truth.

Sacred guides do their work from a place of service and love.

Sacred guides heal themselves and are constantly expanding their own consciousness.

When you need a sacred guide, one is already on its way. Your calling is also an intuition of their arrival.

—————— Invocation ——————

Angels, please give me a clear sign that I will recognise so that I may know my sacred guide when they appear.

Guiding Angels:
Archangel Chamuel, Archangel Raphael, Archangel Zadkiel

DAY 232

Channelled Angel message

You are a radiant expression of love. A miracle awakening now.

You walk, breathe, laugh, and love.

You dance, create, imagine, and build.

Life is born from you. You literally create life from your body and love with another.

You heal, nurse, teach and learn.

You are indeed a miracle.

You are indeed radiant and limitless.

See your full radiance now! Rejoice at your very existence!

We love you infinitely to remind you of your infinite capacity to love.

For remembering your radiance is a journey of awakening to love.

We accept you completely. You have made no mistakes, you have no reason to fear, nor any reason to feel shame.

Every moment of your life has been perfectly created to give you the exact experience required to create the life you are living right now in this moment.

All is here to teach you love of others and of self.

Your awakening to love is the pathway to all that you desire.

————— Invocation —————

Angels, help me awaken to infinite love now. Please help me see
my life as divine perfection in every moment, and release all
regret, shame, and judgement.

Guiding Angels:
Archangel Haniel, Archangel Chamuel, Archangel Zadkiel

DAY 233

Channelled Angel message

You manifest what you are ready for. There is divine perfection in every experience.

The human journey is full spectrum. It is a journey of the exploration of love, via connection and consciousness.

Every experience has meaning. Every experience is a miracle.

That which is painful is also love.

That which is joyful is also love.

One does not know joy without knowing sorrow.

One does not understand overcoming without knowing the struggle.

You chose to experience human life in all its miraculous glory.

You are a conscious participant. This is not something happening to you. You are a part of the miracle.

All that you experience has been miraculously presented to you in order to give you the exact experience you are having now.

Every single action until now has been energetically balanced in perfect equilibrium to create this divine moment.

Indeed, every moment is a miracle of divine perfect balance with all living things, with you at the centre.

All moments are miracles. None are better or worse. They are all equal. They are all glory. They are all grace. They are all love.

Now that you know, we invite you to experience life with wonder and awe.

<hr />

Invocation

Angels, please remind me that everything is in divine perfect order, and that I am experiencing a miracle right now in this moment.

Guiding Angels:
Archangel Uriel, Archangel Faithl, Archangel Jophiel

DAY 234

Channelled Angel message

Divine timing is a miracle. It's ok to let go and wait for the shift.

When you look back at your life until now, has there ever been a time when clarity did not come? Has there ever been a time when you did not experience the shift that you desired?

Can you see now that things have always happened exactly when they were supposed to?

Life is a miracle. You are a miracle.

Every experience, person, event, and occurrence has been created with infinite divine perfection in order to facilitate the collective and individual experience of right now.

Every single occurrence is in divine perfect order.

And so, we invite you to soften and let go.

There has never been a need to push or control your experience.

That which you desire already exists in a now/future reality.

The form and timing of that which you desire manifesting are divine.

The more you soften and open to your experience, the richer your experience becomes.

There is always a shift available to you, even right now, for there is only now.

The shift is within you. It is energetic and heartfelt. It is a shift of awareness and of love.

Letting go is a shift that alters your experience immediately.

Having faith is a shift that opens your energy to receive.

You are the creator. Your letting go becomes an act of love and creation.

Let go now, dear one. There is a magical experience unfolding.

--------- Invocation ---------

Angels, please help me let go and open to the infinite love of the divine. Please remind me that I am safe to trust in the infinite love of the one creator.

Guiding Angels:
Archangel Michael, Archangel Uriel, Archangel Faith

DAY 235

Channelled Angel message

You create change by embodying that which you desire.

There is no need to force. There is no need to change the beliefs of another.

The way is peace. The way is love.

When you feel passion for a cause, for change, for an outcome or for a result, we encourage you to look within.

Where are you out of alignment with your values, integrity, or desires?

What can you shift within your own actions, heart, or beliefs in order to embody that which you are craving?

You are the answer to all that you seek.

You draw that which you desire to you via your alignment.

As you create change in your own reality, your external reality changes, and shifts.

As you become peace, you receive peace.

As you become love, you receive love.

The secret is to become.

This is the most powerful expression of self possible.

You create a new world through changing your inner world.

That is the way of acceptance.

───────── Invocation ─────────

Angels, please show me the pathway to change that lies within so that I may embody that which I desire to see in the world.

Guiding Angels:
Archangel Nathaniel, Archangel Chamuel, Archangel Michael

DAY 236

Channelled Angel message

Practise acceptance as you move through any expansion or growth experience.

As you move into a new pathway, your frequency will expand.

Situations where you once reacted with a closed and protected heart will feel unfamiliar and new.

You are breaking old habits and stepping out of old patterns. This is the pathway of faith.

There is no roadmap, and the old ways no longer work for you.

As your consciousness explores this new frequency and expression, you find everything seems different from this new heart awareness.

Your own awareness shift has opened you to this new pathway. What you see now exists because of your commitment to your healing, and your desire to look beyond your veils.

And so, as you step forwards, we invite you to go gently.

The old ways do not work here. It is meant to feel unfamiliar. It is.

This will be a process of tentative exploration. Of reaching out and pulling back. Of acclimatising.

You require no validation or permission to walk this new path.

All you need is bravery, and acceptance of self. For this is only about you.

Ground now into your heart and know that every step forward is ok.

Soon this place will feel like home.

——————— Invocation ———————

Angels, please assist me through this time of transition and change, especially when I feel uncomfortable.

Guiding Angels: Archangel Nathaniel, Archangel Michael

DAY 237

Channelled Angel message

Everything you see in another is a projection of self. An illusion.

All that you see is a mirror to your own experience.

The behaviour, actions, or words of another that have an impact on you only do so because of your own awareness.

When you feel triggered by another, the pathway to peace lies within.

You have no control over the actions of another.

You have unlimited freedom over your own actions and thoughts.

And so, you shift your experience by shifting your own thoughts, actions, and behaviours.

Every moment is an opportunity for discovery and growth.

Every moment is an opportunity for finding the way home to love.

Every moment is an opportunity for awakening to your own judgements, limiting beliefs, and shadows.

You are your healer, your teacher, and the one who can give you what you desire. You always were.

Awakening to the illusion is both the purpose and the process; it is a practice ongoing.

You are not alone on this journey. Love exists always.

——————— Invocation ———————

Angels, when I feel triggered by the actions or words of another, please help me find peace, acceptance, and forgiveness within.

Guiding Angels: Archangel Zadkiel, Archangel Chamuel

DAY 238

Channelled Angel message

There is no separation of science and spirit. Creation requires both love and mathematical patterns.

As the collective expansion of consciousness occurs, the shifts create new awareness.

This process of birthing 5D consciousness is one of realisation.

Unity is a requirement for 5D consciousness. And so, all that is disunity and divided is now becoming visible.

The division of science and spirit exists both in the individual and collective consciousness.

We ask you; how can one be conscious without understanding that consciousness is both energetic and physical? It is impossible.

You are conscious because you are both a pattern and a miracle.

You are both a scientific process and an expression of miraculous and infinite love.

Your physical existence is able to be understood, measured and explained scientifically, and yet your conscious existence is unable to be explained and understood without faith.

When science began to attempt to explain consciousness, there became two pathways when there was only ever one.

The exploration of these two pathways has yielded the experience of the collective human consciousness until now. This has been necessary. All is as it was meant to be.

And now the pathways merge and join again.

Wayshowers are now reintegrating the physical and the non-physical.

Love is being explored as a unified expression.

This will and is creating an explosion of consciousness.

The full capacity of human expression will be realised via the unification of science and spirit. By a return to oneness, and a reclaiming of divinity.

This pathway is unified within. As you make peace with your own divided self, you anchor 5D unity consciousness for the collective.

This is the most sacred journey, and your very reason for being here now.

An evolution of science and spirit will emerge in the consciousness of all beings now.

——————— Invocation ———————

Angels, please help me explore my own beliefs and understanding about science and spirit so that I might find a unified expression and new pathway within my own consciousness.

Guiding Angels:
Archangel Raziel, Archangel Butyalil, Archangel Metatron

DAY 239

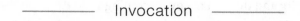
Channelled Angel message

Every moment is a miracle.

Every moment has a purpose.

You are a miracle.

Your very being is the purpose, and all you ever needed to do was that which you love.

As soon as you let go of all the rules and bring your attention to love, to presence, to exploration and to curiosity, all will unfold divinely.

——————— Invocation ———————

Angels, please remind me that my purpose is simply to be myself.

DAY 240

Channelled Angel message

As you begin to explore your heart, you will find all that you have yet to discover.

All that you seek exists within.

The discovery of self is the purpose for existence.

As you discover self, you discover love.

As you discover self, your relationships shift and expand.

As you discover self, your joy, fulfilment, and awareness increase.

What do you like? Follow that pathway.

Where have you taken on beliefs that are not yours?

Where have you shut down your intuition?

Where have you given your power away?

The discovery of self is shadow work, and requires compassion, forgiveness, and acceptance.

As you explore self, you will raise your frequency.

As you follow your joy, you will become all that you desire.

You are the pathway. You are the answer.

—————— Invocation ——————

Angels, please help me on the pathway of discovering all that is hidden so that I can become my full authentic self.

Guiding Angels:
Archangel Nathaniel, Archangel Michael, Archangel Zadkiel

DAY 241

Channelled Angel message

Polarity allows for the exploration of love. Walk towards your triggers to discover a deeper experience of love.

Everything is a mirror offering you a window into your own awareness, healing, and expansion.

Particularly the triggers.

As you become conscious of the desire for a new way, a new earth, we want you to know that the journey is inwards.

Division and polarity are opportunities to explore love via your own consciousness.

Division shows you a pathway of acceptance and forgiveness. This is a miraculous healing journey.

Polarity shows you a pathway of unity and partnership. This is a miraculous healing journey.

And so, look with curiosity and joy at the opportunities being presented to you now.

Have you ever seen more opportunities for the creation of the miracles you desire?

Your healing now is in direct proportion to the collective healing and birth of New Earth.

Invocation

Angels, please help me in the moment to see that triggers of division and polarity are opportunities for discovery, healing, unity, and acceptance.

Guiding Angels:
Archangel Nathaniel, Archangel Metatron,
Archangel Butyalil

DAY 242

Channelled Angel message

Division is showing you the pathway to unity.

You have no control over the actions of another. All you are ever able to see is a reflection of yourself.

As you look at your collective consciousness now and see division, we ask you to look within and notice: where do you feel divided?

As you notice actions of another that trigger you, we ask you to notice where this creates room for embodiment of that which you desired to experience in that situation.

As you see division externally, you also see the opportunity to bring your own body/mind/spirit into harmony and equilibrium.

For the state of the collective is a reflection of the total sum of individuals.

And so, to heal the world, you must heal yourself.

And so, to experience peace, you must look for peace within.

And so, to bring unity to a divided world, you must embody compassion, acceptance, and forgiveness of self and others.

This is the only way.

We invite you to remember your relationship with the divine, and with your own heart.

We invite you to remember that you chose this sacred journey now: to walk within to heal yourself now.

We shall assist you, and the sacred guides that you need will appear at the exact right time.

The time for awakening is now.

——————— Invocation ———————

Angels, please help me find my way through the triggers of my experience to find peace, acceptance, and love within.

DAY 243

Channelled Angel message

What presents as a problem is here to expand your consciousness.

Life presents you with the perfect experience in every moment.

Just because something initially feels like a challenge, problem, or obstacle, does not mean that it is so.

In fact, we ask you to open to the possibility that when you feel triggered, you are in fact being presented with an opportunity for exploration.

Growth exists in this direction. Miracles exist in this direction. Change exists in this direction.

Walk towards that which feels difficult.

Walk towards that which is opening a new pathway, as this situation is in perfect divine order for the growth you desire.

What feels like a problem is in fact a miraculous opportunity for the very outcome you desire. If you let go.

Even challenges are here to teach you. We remind you that you chose these experiences before you incarnated.

The miracle lies this way.

Love lies this way.

Let go now; you are safe to explore and investigate this new experience.

—————— Invocation ——————

Angels, please remind me that my most difficult challenges are actually my most incredible opportunities for miraculous growth.

Guiding Angels: Archangel Faith, Archangel Metatron

DAY 244

Channelled Angel message

Everything teaches you something. Love is in every moment.

There is divine perfection in every experience.

All moments are orchestrated miraculously to give you the experience you are having now.

This is a miracle.

How can a positive experience be a miracle and a negative one not be?

All moments are miraculous.

All moments require the same breath of life, the same energetic interplay of a multitude of interesting moments.

All moments are divine.

All moments are love.

Look for the love in this moment. We will assist you and whisper the way.

——————— Invocation ———————

Angels, please remind me that all experiences are miracles, so that I can let go and be present to the miracle occurring right now.

Guiding Angels: Archangel Faith, Archangel Uriel

DAY 245

Channelled Angel message

We remove obstacles from your path for a reason. Have faith in the process.

That which you seek exists and it will manifest into form at the exact right moment.

There is perfection in the timing, and the journey from here to there is both the purpose and the pathway of creating that which you desire.

Every step in the journey is a part of the plan, even the experiences that do not work out as you expect or seem to redirect you.

Each moment shows you that which you love, and that which you don't love. Both help you express yourself in alignment with your own heart frequency.

And so, when some experiences feel like mistakes or unsuccessful, we ask you to shift your perspective.

All moments have a reason, and the ones that do not work as you expect are here to take you to that which is in resonance with you.

That which is in resonance with you will come at the moment you are in frequency alignment.

And so, your job is to bring yourself into frequency alignment with that which you desire.

And so, let go of the things that do not work out, as they are part of the plan to bring you that which you desire.

—————— Invocation ——————

Angels, as one doorway closes, please remind me that this creates room for a brand-new experience that is in alignment with my highest good. Please remind me that all experiences are perfect, and that there are no mistakes.

Guiding Angels:
Archangel Nathaniel, Archangel Faith, Archangel Michael

DAY 246

Channelled Angel message

Creation requires desire and faith.

As you focus on manifesting your desire, we ask you to let go.

Attachment does not harmonise your frequency with that which you desire.

Attachment contracts your frequency and narrows your focal point.

That which you desire is a feeling, and your heart is both a powerful generator and attractor.

In order to harmonise your frequency with the frequency of that which you desire, all you need to do is feel your way there.

Spend time imagining and daydreaming.

This is creation.

Creation is generating feelings of love in your heart that harmonise your frequency to that which you desire.

Daydreaming is creation. Imagining is creation.

This is manifestation.

―――――――― Invocation ――――――――

Angels, please remind me to let go of expectations and focus on appreciation, desire and love as I allow myself to become that which I desire.

Guiding Angels:
Archangel Ariel, Archangel Faith, Archangel Metatron

DAY 247

Channelled Angel message

The transition to New Earth occurs within. Heal disunity within your own body/mind/spirit.

The transition to New Earth is underway, with light codes activating the transition phase now.

These light codes highlight all that exists within your body/mind/spirit complex that is not integrated or healed and is still experienced as disunity or separation within your own consciousness.

In order for New Earth to transition to unity consciousness, unity must first be embodied within.

Unity without occurs in direct proportion to and as a result of unity within.

And so, we ask you to notice all that presents as disunity and separation outside of yourself and use this as an opportunity to explore disunity and separation within your own mind/body/spirit.

For all that you see outside of yourself is only a mirror of your inner reality.

Do you desire peace? Seek peace within.

Do you desire harmony? Seek harmony within.

Do you desire love? Seek love within.

Do you notice unhealed and toxic behaviour in others? Explore the unhealed and toxic behaviour within.

——————— Invocation ———————

Angels, please remind me that all that I see is but a
mirror of my own soul.

Guiding Angels:
Archangel Metatron, Archangel Butyalil, Archangel Chamuel

DAY 248

Channelled Angel message

As you love and celebrate the divine masculine, the divine masculine loves and celebrates you.

We invite you to celebrate and love the divine masculine as it appears in your experience.

We remind you that the love you give is the love you receive, in all things.

And so, if you feel unloved, hurt, controlled, or victimised by the divine masculine, we ask you to know that this is healed within.

Give love, peace, freedom, and acceptance to the divine masculine as it is present in your life to restore balance and harmony to your experience of and with the masculine.

Love creates love.

You are your expression of the divine masculine, and you can re-calibrate your energy to match that which you desire to experience in frequency interaction with the divine masculine.

There is no toxic masculinity. There is only unhealed humans experiencing consciousness.

Harmony and balance with both the feminine and masculine is found within.

Become that which you desire to experience by giving it without need of receiving.

────────── Invocation ──────────

Angels, please show me the pathway to unifying my experience of both the masculine and feminine so that I may both give and receive love without resistance.

Guiding Angels: Archangel Haniel, Archangel Nathaniel

DAY 249

Channelled Angel message

Anger towards another is anger towards self.

There is nothing wrong with anger, or any other emotion. All emotions and feelings have a purpose.

All emotions and feelings are a message allowing you to understand your own consciousness.

Anger shows you a pathway within, to explore your own triggers.

When you feel anger towards another, we invite you to become curious and feel safe exploring your own feelings.

Anger towards another is a gateway to understanding where you are holding anger towards yourself.

Begin here. Become mindful of your expression and words towards others. When you notice the temptation to express anger towards another, pause, become curious.

Sacred anger is healthy.

We do not ask you to contain your anger; we ask you to become mindful and accountable in your expression of anger.

Peace is found in full acceptance of all emotions, including anger.

——————— Invocation ———————

Angels, please help me find peace and acceptance with my shadow feelings so that I can feel safe expressing my anger.

Guiding Angels:
Archangel Raguel, Archangel Chamuel, Archangel Zadkiel

DAY 250

Channelled Angel message

The world is changed by you.

All that you desire is within your grasp right now.

All the change that you see possible in your outer-world reality is created within your inner-world reality.

For you are not separate from your outer or inner realities. You are one. There is one reality.

Your perception and awareness are all that is.

You are all that is.

And so, as you look outside and desire change, we invite you to look within to create the change that you desire.

As you look outside and see grief, trauma, disease, toxicity, and imbalance, we ask you to look within to heal grief, trauma, disease, toxicity, and imbalance.

Your highest priority is your own healing and transformation. As you heal yourself, you heal the world.

——————— Invocation ———————

Angels, please show me the pathway to change
and healing within.

Guiding Angels:
Archangel Raphael, Archangel Zadkiel, Archangel Nathaniel

DAY 251

Channelled Angel message

Your human experience is full spectrum. Allow yourself full expression.

Your purpose is to explore love.

Love is full spectrum.

Every human emotion and every experience have a divine perfect purpose, at the exact divine moment, to give you your journey to explore love.

All that you are exists to be explored and expressed.

The outward spiral expansion of consciousness occurs with unconditional acceptance of the shadow aspects of self.

Everything exists in polarity. Everything exists in perfect balance. Everything is an experience of love.

So, allow yourself to be both joyful and sad. To laugh and cry. To feel peace and rage. And know that you are accepted by the universal one consciousness of creation simply because you exist.

And know that the moment you soften into full acceptance of all aspects of your own self, you become enlightened.

Enlightenment is acceptance of self.

Enlightenment is acceptance of love.

You are loved and you are love.

--------- Invocation ---------

Angels, please help me practise acceptance of all aspects of myself so that I can realise my full expression of being.

Guiding Angels: Archangel Nathaniel, Archangel Chamuel

DAY 252

Channelled Angel message

Shifts happen when you let go and allow the divine to speak through you.

The belief that you are separate from the divine creates a state of tension.

In truth, you are infinitely loved and supported by the divine, always.

All the shifts that you desire exist now, in this moment, as you realise and recall that you are the creator and that your awareness creates your reality.

Realisation is the moment of reconnection with the divine.

Your miracle occurs as you see what has always been.

You are one. We are one. There is no division.

And so, we remind you to let go.

Let your body soften into circuitry with all that is a part of and an extension of you.

The divine is speaking to you and through you in every moment. Are you ready to listen? It is the language of love, it is harmonic frequency, and it is here, now, in your heart.

────── Invocation ──────

I am one with the divine, and with all living beings.
I am the creator, I am love.

Guiding Angels: Archangel Uriel

DAY 253

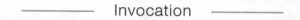
Channelled Angel message

Become that which you seek.

All that you see in the world is changed by your own actions.

As you see anger, become peace.

As you see division, become unity.

As you see hatred, become love.

As you see greed, become generosity.

As you see fear, become trust.

And so, when you desire change, become that which you desire.

For this was always the way.

Angels, please help me see that everything is a mirror to guide my path to realisation and expansion of consciousness.

Guiding Angels: Archangel Haniel, Archangel Metatron

DAY 254

Channelled Angel message

Who told you that you need scientific proof that we exist?

We invite you to begin to question that which you know to be true.

You are the master of your reality. Your experience of truth is subject only to your own beliefs, perceptions, experiences, and awareness.

The expansion of human consciousness is an exploration of reality.

Something exists the moment it is imagined.

Something exists the moment it is felt.

This is the beginning of the creation process, and you are the creator.

Angels exist the moment you realise that we do. This is when your relationship with us begins.

Your heart guides you to your truth and to us.

Angels, I know you are with me.

Guiding Angels: Archangel Uriel Archangel Faith

DAY 255

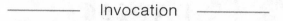
Channelled Angel message

Everything you seek exists within. The moment you realise this, everything changes.

You need no permission.

You need no validation.

You need no acceptance.

You need no love.

All that you look for outside yourself exists within.

As you give yourself permission, as you accept yourself, as you love yourself, as you approve of and feel proud of yourself, all that you seek begins to be reflected back to you from the outside.

It is all a mirror.

It is all a match to your frequency.

And so, now that you know, the only thing left to do is become your fully expressed self.

———— Invocation ————

Angels, please give me clear reminders to look within for
all that I seek externally.

Guiding Angels: Guardian Angels

DAY 256

Channelled Angel message

The current shift requires an inversion of your reality.

What are your beliefs? What do you identify with? What facts, structures, ideologies, mythologies, labels, and values make up your identification of self?

The shift occurring now will turn everything on its head.

All that you know to be true will be flagged for you to re-evaluate.

As you engage with someone in your life or world, we invite you to become curious about your labels for this person. Are they true? Are they a story that you have made up? Are they a story that you have been told by the collective?

Is your experience of trauma creating this projection?

Is your identification with the collective creating this projection?

Is it your truth?

Curiosity is the gateway to identifying and awakening your own sacred and powerful truth.

The spell is being broken now.

Your current process may feel like the most difficult yet, as all you see and believe will morph, shimmer, and come into sudden focus and clarity.

You are powerful. Your heart knows the way forwards here. You are supported by the light as you grow, explore, and change now.

You are safe to see yourself and the world with clarity now.

—————— Invocation ——————

Angels, please show me that which I can't see. Please remove all veils so that I can see myself and the world clearly.

DAY 257

Channelled Angel message

You are an energetic being and require regular physical connection with the earth.

All that you need comes to you via energetic attraction when you are in frequency alignment.

When you feel out of sorts, it is your frequency that has become distorted or inharmonious.

This is not bad. It is a part of the human experience.

When you identify that you feel out of sorts/out of alignment, this is the first step towards growth and healing. The awareness takes you into discovery and exploration of love, polarity, and duality.

Your exploration of distortion and shadow is in equal proportion to your exploration of alignment and light.

You are able to immediately shift your energy and realign with the frequency of light/love by bringing your body into contact with Gaia.

The earth's energy is here to support you unconditionally through every aspect of your human experience.

Let the frequency of the earth work with you and for you as you move through your cycles of expansion and contraction.

———————— Invocation ————————

Angels, please remind me of the constant and unconditional
energetic support from Mother Gaia available to me.

DAY 258

Channelled Angel message

In the quiet, you find your power.

When you feel confused, overwhelmed and out of sync, the peace you seek is found in solitude.

The world you experience now is filled with noise, sound, vibrations, visual stimuli, and other distractions.

This noise, especially frequency noise from electronics, distorts your energy field.

This will present for you as overwhelm, tiredness, lack of clarity, and heightened emotions.

In order to re-calibrate your field, please go to nature and create a silent space.

Your power is your energy.

Re-calibrate to the Gaia field to come back into your power.

———————— Invocation ————————

Angels, please help me become aware of all the different external stimuli that are impacting my energetic field and inner peace.

Guiding Angels:
Archangel Gersisa, Archangel Metatron, Archangel Michael

DAY 259

Channelled Angel message

Your frequency changes with all that you interact with.

Your harmony is not fixed.

This experience of consciousness gifts you a spectrum of miraculous interactions with all that is an expression of conscious love.

Your awareness shifts in exploration of every experience.

This is done through energy.

Your energetic interaction is that which creates an experience first, and is then processed as physical, emotional, and spiritual.

And so, we encourage you to become aware that everything is for a purpose, and that your frequency shifts are in perfect order.

Your frequency will contract and expand, lower, and raise. All is divinely perfect. You learn about love via exploration of polarity and duality, and this is only possible with a full-spectrum frequency and physical experience.

And so, you are also able to consciously steer your experience and shift your frequency. At any time, you can explore a higher frequency of love and light.

As you identify that your experience has included lower vibration or contractions, you learn and expand your consciousness to include this frequency as part of your complete energy/light body memory and record.

Accepting all energy as perfect and integrating all as a divine part of your experience is both the purpose and the pathway.

——————— Invocation ———————

Angels, please help me become aware of my ability to be a finely tuned conductor, receiver and transmitter of energy. Please help me begin to work with the energy I feel, and to intentionally shift my own energy.

DAY 260

Channelled Angel message

When something feels difficult, try looking at it from the opposite perspective.

There is a current inversion of your reality occurring now.

All that you see is being revealed as otherwise. This is the period of the great reveal. This is a time of revelation.

This experience occurs through you, within you.

Your own awareness shifts and as you understand things from a different perspective, the collective consciousness shifts.

As you become aware of the multitude of pathways available to you now, your own experience makes a quantum leap in consciousness.

This shift is monumental both for you and for the collective.

It will feel intense for you at times until you realise that it is not. The solution is available instantly via inversion of your perspective to include unity with the other you are identifying with.

Unity is the way. Your awareness creates the change you desire.

———————— Invocation ————————

Angels, please help me experience a mini quantum leap in my own awareness when I am triggered by an external experience.

Guiding Angels:
Archangel Haniel, Archangel Metatron, Archangel Butyalil

DAY 261

Channelled Angel message

Everything that you see in the world that causes you pain is healed within.

Your reality and your experience are all that exists.

There is nothing else causing you pain. There is only your awareness.

As you change your awareness, you change your experience.

Love exists in every moment. Even when there appears to be an absence of love, there is love to be found via acceptance and compassion for self and 'other' in this moment.

What you see becomes your reality, and you have the power to change your story in every single moment.

Pay attention to your focus. As you identify that which causes you pain, distress, worry or anger, we invite you to become curious.

How can I change this experience?

The change you desire occurs not by waiting for the world to change, but by becoming the peace, love, and joy that you seek.

In every moment, there are an infinite number of alternate pathways available to you. You are the creator and miracles exist in every moment.

Your very existence is proof of miracles.

There is no other causing you pain.

You are sovereign and you are that which you seek.

———————— Invocation ————————

Angels, please remind me that I am the key to the happiness I seek.
All answers are within.

Guiding Angels:
Archangel Faith, Archangel Haniel, Archangel Jophiel

DAY 262

Channelled Angel message

Your imagination is the key to the creation of your desires.

The creation process that you understand as manifesting is one of energy.

Your mind is the computer that generates an energetic charge that interacts with what you desire.

This charge is an attractor. It works as a magnet and draws that which you desire towards you.

And so, it is simple.

Daydream. Imagine. And feel.

Play with your mind. Have fun with this process. Spend time daydreaming your desires into reality.

Because life isn't always so serious. And creation isn't always so hard.

────── Invocation ──────

Angels, please remind me that co-creation is magical,
joyous, and fun.

Guiding Angels: Archangel Jophiel, Archangel Ariel

DAY 263

Channelled Angel message

Every answer that you seek is found within. Seek teachers who direct your attention inwards.

A good teacher is merely a catalyst to your own journey of self-discovery, of finding knowledge, and of healing.

All true sacred guides understand this, and you will feel activated and empowered when working with a guide who is in service to light.

You are one with the universal consciousness. You are not separate.

All the information you seek—the answers and the guidance—comes to you in divine timing and is felt within.

Any who seeks to control this journey is not a sacred guide and is reflecting to you in that moment an opportunity for you to learn about sovereignty.

Your intuition—your ability to receive guidance and connect with the divine source of love and infinite creation—is limitless.

You awaken to your powerful intuition, your ability to heal, and your sovereignty the moment you become curious about it.

―――――― Invocation ――――――

Angels, please help me practise discernment as I work with sacred guides, and always seek answers within.

Guiding Angels: Archangel Michael, Archangel Raphael

DAY 264

Channelled Angel message

There is no other. Whoever is in your path is there for a reason, as a mirror.

Each interaction is divinely orchestrated with perfection for the exact situation required for your learning experience.

There are no coincidences.

All moments are perfect. All people are presented to you in perfect timing. All experiences gift you exactly what you need to learn in that moment.

The person you are interacting with is not your enemy. They are not here to control you, hurt you or take advantage of you.

Every human interaction is one that gifts you an experience of love, in relationship.

There is only a mirror to your own experience that plays out. There is only yourself in reflection. There is only your own perception. There is only ever now, and there is only ever love in all its shades.

Begin to look at all people as part of yourself and explore the gifts that they bring to you, and everything will change. This applies to all people, no matter how removed they seem to you.

Love is everywhere. Look for it and you will find it, within yourself.

—————— Invocation ——————

Angels, please help me shift my perception of my human experience so that I can feel the love and miracles in every moment.

Guiding Angels:
Archangel Chamuel, Archangel Uriel, Archangel Metatron

DAY 265

Channelled Angel message

There are no mistakes. There is divine perfection in every moment.

Everything has been created in perfect divine order. The same loving intelligence that creates stars, butterflies, flowers, and you, created the exact moment you are experiencing now.

And so, rather than asking *Why is this happening to me?* We encourage you to become curious.

What can you learn about love, about yourself, about life from this current experience?

What are you missing? What is happening here that you can't see that will give you the breakthrough or experience you desire?

There are no mistakes. You are not doing anything wrong. Every moment is an opportunity for a miracle—in fact, every moment is a miracle.

And so, be curious, have fun, and play with your current situation.

We will guide and assist you, all you need to do is ask.

We love and accept you exactly as you are.

————— Invocation —————

Angels, please show me the gifts in the experience
I am having right now.

Guiding Angels:
Archangel Haniel, Archangel Faith, Archangel Jophiel

DAY 266

Channelled Angel message

Wait. Clarity comes in divine timing.

You will at times feel as though you are moving through different worlds now.

And you are.

There is a great shift occurring now.

There are two different vibrational frequencies and realities occurring at once.

There are two different levels of consciousness being explored at once (through your experience and through the collective, for both are the same).

At times, this can feel confusing, overwhelming, even uncomfortable.

3D consciousness asks you to push, take action, and control your process. It is fear based, separation based and lack based.

5D consciousness invites you to get curious, explore with love, let go of beliefs, and discover a new reality. 5D asks you to embody that which you seek, and express unity.

And so, we invite you to know that as you shift between these two realities, the clarity and shift that you desire will come exactly when it's meant to, and that this experience is important to honour in all its moments.

All is as it should be.

—————— Invocation ——————

Angels, please remind me that I am exactly where I am meant to be, and that I am safe to let go and be in this moment.

Guiding Angels:
Archangel Haniel, Archangel Faith, Archangel Metatron

DAY 267

Channelled Angel message

Everything you see in another exists within you.

There is no other.

There is only your own experience of reality.

There is only a mirror to show you your own exploration of love.

There is only your own anger, rage, sadness, impatience, abuse, intolerance, racism, sexism, and all other judgements.

All intolerance, separation and division only exist within you until the moment you realise your power and let it go.

The moment you realise you are not a victim, your perspective shifts and your power is recalled.

Everything can shift in an instant.

———— Invocation ————

Angels, please remind me that my perception is the key to changing my reality in an instant.

Guiding Angels:
Archangel Jophiel, Archangel Metatron, Archangel Butyalil

DAY 268

Channelled Angel message

People come into your life at the exact right moment.

Not a moment before.

Each person you interact with has a purpose.

Each relationship is there to activate your experience of love.

This applies to every single interaction. Even the fleeting ones.

Everything is divinely orchestrated.

There are no mistakes.

You do not need to force any interaction. All you need to do is be yourself, be curious, and trust your own guidance.

You will know when something needs to be explored. And equally you will know when a soul contract has ended.

Let go and trust the energetic messages you are always receiving.

———— Invocation ————

Angels, please help me learn to trust my own powerful heart guidance, and to let go.

DAY 269

Channelled Angel message

You become that which you seek when you realise that you are ready.

The becoming is energetic and instant.

Your shift occurs at the divine right moment, as all components, people and experiences align spontaneously to create your shift.

And so, all you need to do is notice, be, and feel.

Your curiosity and inquiry are the pathway to becoming and to creation.

Your journey inwards is your pathway to the shift and all that you desire.

And so, let go and allow yourself to blossom, and be now.

———————— Invocation ————————

Angels, please remind me to let go and be curious
right now in this moment.

Guiding Angels:
Archangel Jeremiel, Archangel Jophiel, Archangel Haniel

DAY 270

Channelled Angel message

Your imagination is your magic wand. You are the magician.

You are only limited by your imagination.

The limits are of your own making and breaking.

You create with energy that is activated in your pineal gland.

In order to create all that you desire, and live a radiant, expansive life of joy, all you need to do is become all that you love.

Imagine your way to all that you desire. Do this with wonder, with awe, with gratitude and with detachment.

Play with your creation. Let yourself explore your dreams and try them on for size to see how they feel.

And so, we ask you to honour your dreams and ideas, to honour your imagination, to feed it and nurture it, and listen to your heart in the process.

Let love activate your imagination rather than fear. This component is vital. And be wary of any who incites fear intentionally.

Invocation

Angels, please help me realise the power of my heart and my imagination to co-create miracles.

Guiding Angels:
Archangel Metatron, Archangel Uriel, Archangel Faith

DAY 271

Channelled Angel message

When you explore life from a place of joy and curiosity, there are no mistakes.

Every experience is an opportunity to learn about love.

The journey of being human can feel difficult at times.

To shift your experience, we encourage you to soften into curious and joyful exploration.

How can I shift this experience?

What am I missing here?

Where can I find more joy in this experience?

There is always guidance available to you, within your own heart, and from us.

Our guidance is only ever a mirror of your own heart, as we do not violate your free will.

Your heart is your most powerful guide, and joy is available for you as soon as you seek it.

—————— Invocation ——————

Angels, please help me see and feel the love that exists in this moment.

Guiding Angels:
Archangel Chamuel, Archangel Jophiel, Archangel Grace

DAY 272

Channelled Angel message

The answer is always in your heart.

Every answer you seek can be felt.

Love is always your guide.

When things feel easy, when you feel sure, when you feel joyful, excited, and eager, then you will know. Until then, wait and trust.

Your heart never guides you astray.

Your heart is sensitive and energetic. It is powerful beyond belief. It is both a magnet and an energy conductor.

Your heart in harmony with your imagination will create miracles and manifest instantly all that you desire.

Opening your heart and learning your heart language requires trust and faith. It requires silencing the voices outside of yourself so that you remember your own inner love language.

This sovereign heart journey is sacred, and can be assisted by a sacred guide, healer or teacher. Someone who empowers you to turn within, who does not give you the answers but reminds you that you have the answers.

We can also assist you.

―――――― Invocation ――――――

Angels, please help me begin to open my heart, and learn to listen to my own sacred heart language.

Guiding Angels:
Archangel Chamuel, Archangel Faith, Archangel Haniel

DAY 273

Channelled Angel message

Your heart is opening to love now. You are safe.

This is a significant energetic shift.

Your shift is a heart expansion that will open your energy, mind, and body to a different experience of love.

Your understanding of love is changing now as your frequency rises.

The energy of light/love is flooding through you at a high rate.

This may feel uncomfortable at times. It will equally feel easy, calm, and safe at times.

The guidance you seek through this transition to a higher love experience will be found within.

Your heart is the transmitter and receiver, and it will show you with its love pulsations how to navigate this shift.

This shift is felt. It is a heart shift. It cannot be understood with logic, planning, or thinking.

Allow yourself space to move through this shift with curiosity, and without attachment or control.

The breakthroughs you desire can be found on the other side of this heart shift.

———————— Invocation ————————

Angels, please help me feel safe as I experience my heart awakening.

Guiding Angels:
Archangel Chamuel, Archangel Michael, Archangel Raphael

DAY 274
Channelled Angel message

It is time to look at everything with a new lens.

All is not as it seems.

Your awareness is changing now as the amount of light/love frequency is increasing.

As you open your heart chakra and attune your energy to light/love, you recall you are one with the universal consciousness.

As this awareness occurs, your perception shifts.

As your perception shifts, the veil thins, and you become aware that all you understood to be true has been understood through a filter.

As this filter shifts, you become aware of knowing nothing.

As you become aware of knowing nothing, you become aware of the need to know nothing.

And so, you become aware that love is all that exists and that your capacity to love is limitless, for you are love.

All that you desire becomes accessible to you as you become

aware that you are indeed the creator, and that love is your creation tool.

And so, all you need do is observe, enquire, and love.

——————— Invocation ———————

Angels, please remind me that I know nothing, and that all I need to do is experience love.

Guiding Angels:
Archangel Chamuel, Archangel Uriel, Archangel Faith

DAY 275

Channelled Angel message

As the veil thins, your sensitivity increases. This is your natural state.

You may notice energetic sensations moving through your body, heightened emotions, and a feeling of intensity to your experience.

You may notice your intuition increase significantly.

You may notice things look different in your surroundings.

You may notice that you feel a heart connection to others more easily.

You may notice you are receiving guidance from us more easily.

You may notice you are able to feel and hear communication from other energetic beings now.

You may notice your connection to your ancestors is becoming stronger.

You may notice a strong pull to connect closely with those you have a blood relationship with, and that other relationships become either instantly stronger or instantly more distant.

As the veil thins, all distortions and shadows are being revealed, and your heart frequency is increasing.

Trust the signs, connections, and messages you are receiving now, even if they take you in unexpected directions.

Trust that which feels familiar and easy. That which feels like love.

Also walk towards that which feels difficult but guided, as this is your shadow work and healing.

You will acclimatise to this new sensitivity. In fact, you will learn to use your sensitivities, for they are a part of your natural state.

This language is one you remember. It is the language of energy, of light/love.

—————— Invocation ——————

Angels, please help me adjust to experiencing life with an open heart.

Guiding Angels:
Archangel Chamuel, Archangel Raphael, Archangel Haniel

DAY 276

Channelled Angel message

You can shift your experience by returning to love in any moment.

Love is always present, even when it feels as if it is not.

When you feel angry, sad, disconnected, lonely, frustrated or any other challenging emotion, we invite you to look for love.

The shift you seek, the answers you seek, will present themselves to you as soon as you begin to shift your focus and look for them.

The answers are always within.

Your heart is always the messenger, and the shift will come as soon as you ask your heart for guidance.

Notice your energy drop into your body. Notice your heart open and soften. Notice the feeling of love returning and spreading through you, growing until you feel overcome with love.

This feeling is always available to you, with conscious and intentional thought.

We will assist you to return your energy to your heart and to love in any moment when you ask.

We do not do this, you do. You are the heart magician. We merely reflect back the love you feel, and then it amplifies.

Invocation

Angels, please help me experience a shift in this moment to love.

Guiding Angels:
Archangel Chamuel, Archangel Metatron, Archangel Butyalil

DAY 277

Channelled Angel message

This is a time of great transformation and change. Just not in the way you expect.

Even though you see great changes occurring in the world now, this has always been the case. Change has always occurred.

So why does this experience feel more intense, seem different, and seem like great change is occurring at a rapid speed?

The change and transformation that is occurring is one of perception. One of consciousness. One of awareness.

Your perception of reality is changing.

What you knew to be 'true' is now something that you are questioning. And this seems to be occurring in the world around you.

Everything that you saw as fixed is now fluid.

The things that helped you understand yourself and your place in the world are now things that you are questioning.

And so, go gently.

This time is one where all is inverted.

Shadows are revealed and veils are removed.

All this happens within.

Your heart will guide you through this experience and help you find a new way of looking at the world that is softer, more compassionate, more loving, and more connected.

This is the miracle transformation. Of birth.

This shift is a return to your fully expanded living state. To a state of love/light.

And so, along the way you will see all that was hidden.

Compassion for self is your pathway through this experience. Self-love is your pathway through this experience. Acceptance is the pathway through this experience.

——————— Invocation ———————

Angels, please help me practise compassion, acceptance, forgiveness and unconditional love for self as I navigate my own inversion of consciousness.

Guiding Angels:
Archangel Zadkiel, Archangel Haniel, Archangel Metatron

DAY 278

Channelled Angel message

Nothing is as it seems. It is only as you see it.

Everything about your experience now is to show you your

own veils.

Everything about your experience now is to show you your filters, your limiting beliefs, your stories, your shadows, and your false and true identity.

As you become aware of your filters, you also become aware of how to remove them.

As you become aware of your beliefs, you also become aware of the ability to change them.

As you become aware of your story, you also become able to change it.

As you become aware, you discover and reclaim hidden parts of yourself.

As you become aware, your perception shifts, and distortions become clear.

As you become aware, you become detached and more centred in your heart.

This is the shift. It is the remembering that love is all that matters. It is the remembering of your sovereignty, your power, your radiance, your ability to learn by following your powerful heart wisdom.

Your intuition is becoming your guide now.

Your heart is becoming your guide now.

You are awakening to the infinite love that is within all beings and within you, for you are not separate from the divine, or from any other.

——————— Invocation ———————

Angels, be by my side as I adjust to a complete inversion of my reality and sense of self.

Guiding Angels:
Archangel Michael, Archangel Metatron,
Archangel Nathaniel

DAY 279

Channelled Angel message

You are experiencing a return to sovereignty of body, mind, and spirit.

The current shift is an inversion of consciousness.

You are being asked to identify where your power has been given over to an authority outside of yourself.

In every aspect of life, there is potential for authority. Someone or something outside of yourself who you turn to for guidance, healing, validation, education, and governance.

And yet, you are sovereign.

And so, you are always able to know your pathway and find your answers, and navigate your healing, education, life decisions and all aspects of your life.

No other knows you.

No other can govern you.

You are free the moment you realise you are free.

You are genius, creative, miraculous, powerful, and special.

Everything you feel and desire is worth exploring.

There are no rules you need to follow. Rules are made up and exist only when you believe them to be true.

Energy always guides you, and when it flows and feels easy, that is your harmonic resonance guiding you to listen and follow that feeling.

You are reclaiming all aspects of your body, mind, and spirit that you have not given voice to, or that you have given over to another.

Be playful and rebellious in your exploration now. This is a powerful reclamation, and it is joyful!

Angels, please assist me as I awaken and recall my radiant and innate power!

Guiding Angels: Archangel Michael

DAY 280

Channelled Angel message

All you need to do is be you.

And we want you to know that the journey to finding, becoming, and expressing all parts of you will feel at times like the most challenging one you will take.

This journey uncovers all the places where you have taken on beliefs, identities and stories from outside of yourself, from the collective consciousness, from the media, from the government, from your family of origin, and from the world around you.

And the journey of discovery of self is one that shows you all the ways and places that you are shrinking, being small, being quiet or choosing to not rock the boat.

And the journey of becoming yourself, or a more expanded version of yourself, requires you to make new choices, set boundaries, believe in your worth, and be brave and fearless in your exploration of joy.

We remind you that this journey is one that is both challenging and rewarding.

This journey is the answer to all that you seek. This journey is your purpose and your awakening.

How can I be more myself? What do I love? What do I not love?

These questions will unlock your pathway to self-actualisation. Your journey home, to you.

Angels, please help me take the first step on the journey
of self-actualisation.

Guiding Angels:
Archangel Metatron, Archangel Jophiel, Archangel Nathaniel

DAY 281

Channelled Angel message

Be discerning about any message that is fear based.

Remember that your heart is an energy transmitter and receiver.

Your heart will never lead you astray.

Your heart will warn you when a message, person or situation is not aligned with your highest good.

Your heart speaks to you with energy, with feelings and with knowing.

Learning to trust your heart requires you to become curious about the information you receive.

Just because someone or something seems to be in a position of authority, does not mean that they know what is best for you. Only you know this.

You are a powerful, radiant, sovereign being!

Be especially mindful of any message that says that you do not know your own mind, and to give your sovereign power of body, mind, or spirit away to another.

It is hard to begin to trust your inner heart wisdom. And you are ready.

We will assist you.

Angels, please assist me as I become discerning and aware of external fear-based messages and begin to awaken to my own inner authority.

Guiding Angels: Archangel Michael, Archangel Haniel

DAY 282

Channelled Angel message

You are safe to connect with the divine.

You need no intermediary to connect with the divine, with God or with your Angelic team.

There is nothing to fear in connecting with the divine or with your Angels.

The divine accepts you exactly as you are.

We accept you exactly as you are.

The divine loves you infinitely.

Any story that causes you to fear judgement, to feel shame or to experience disappointment from the divine is a distortion/projection.

You are infinitely loveable, infinitely capable, infinitely worthy, infinitely radiant.

Your way to the divine, and to us, is via your heart.

Your strong heart wisdom is awakening now.

You will feel the divine, and us, in love.

Search for us where you know love to be.

———— Invocation ————

Angels, please help me heal my relationship with God, with Angels and with the divine.

DAY 283

Channelled Angel message

Joy, peace, and abundance come when you let go.

Everything changes when you let go.

Your heart is always able to guide you.

When things feel constricted, forced or blocked, this is your heart energy speaking to you to let you know that there is another pathway available to you.

This pathway is one of flow.

This pathway is one that requires you to listen to the sacred heart wisdom within.

This pathway exists as a constant state for you to access.

This pathway is the natural flow of the universe.

This pathway is one of faith, one that only you know, one that is uniquely you.

This pathway asks you to trust that you are safe to go gently and to flow with the energy that is asking you now to let go.

———— Invocation ————

Angels, please help me let go and trust the energy of the experience I am having right now in this moment.

Guiding Angels:
Archangel Haniel, Archangel Faith, Archangel Michael

DAY 284

Channelled Angel message

Love is a flowing state. Fear is a controlled state.

Love is intuition, energy, ease, compassion, and trust.

Fear is rules, authority, structure, attachment, and force.

Flow is a state of peaceful allowing. Love is trusting the energy of source.

Fear is forcing. Control is disconnected from source.

Find your flow by remembering that everything operates on the energy of love.

Intuition is love.

Intuition is decisions made without knowing why. Without logic, without reason and without proof.

---— Invocation ——---

Angels, please help me let go and open to the infinite miracles of the divine, which are found only when I open to receive them.

Guiding Angels:
Archangel Haniel, Archangel Michael, Archangel Uriel

DAY 285

Channelled Angel message

All will become clear at the exact right moment.

It's ok to not know.

It's ok to let go.

It's ok to trust in the divine order of things, in the miraculous flow of energy that connects you to all that you desire.

Everything is divine perfection.

That which you desire is forming. There is a purpose in this time in between that you do not understand.

Things always change.

Clarity always comes.

We invite you to explore the idea of trust and faith in yourself. In the universe. In us. In God.

Everything was created perfectly for right now. Let go and allow yourself to experience this moment with gratitude and faith.

─────────── Invocation ───────────

*Angels, please help me let go and trust that I am
exactly where I need to be.*

Guiding Angels: Archangel Faith, Archangel Michael

DAY 286

Channelled Angel message

All conflict is resolved within.

All anger and rage towards another are gateways to peace within.

Conflict can be dissolved instantly once you reframe your experience and perspective.

There is nothing wrong with conflict. There is nothing wrong with anger. These exist in balance and polarity to their opposite counterparts to create a full-spectrum experience of love.

Avoidance of anger and conflict creates imbalances and disharmony within.

Peace and love are always available to you, and connection and expression are the pathway to finding this.

How can you connect with that which causes you anger?

How can you connect with the heart of the person with whom you are feeling anger or rage? This applies to every experience, whether the person is immediate or distant in relationships (including government or public figures).

Remembering that they are but an aspect of you is the beginning.

Find empathy, acceptance, and forgiveness within, and you find it for another.

——————— Invocation ———————

Angels, please help me connect with those who I feel anger towards so that I can feel safe to express my anger and find peace within.

Guiding Angels:
Archangel Zadkiel, Archangel Chamuel, Archangel Raguel

DAY 287

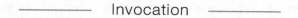
Channelled Angel message

All is not as it seems. It is better.

As the veil thins now, you will become more aware and open to the collective energy.

At times, you may notice a pervasive consciousness of fear within the collective.

This is both unconscious and conscious.

You are a highly tuned energetic being who is capable of intuiting the energy and emotions of others and the collective.

We invite you to become curious now. Is this sensation mine? Does it feel true to me? Do I resonate with this energy?

This is how you fine-tune your own energetic antenna.

Nothing is ever as bad as it seems. It is always much better. Becoming skilled at discerning the truth of a situation, feeling or experience requires trust, faith, and inner inquiry.

Everyone has the ability to develop their energetic and visual intuitive abilities.

It is easier now than ever.

We can assist you with this in a way that feels natural and safe.

———— Invocation ————

Angels, please help me strengthen my energetic intuition so that I can learn to discern where my energy ends and hold boundaries with the collective energy and energy of other beings.

Guiding Angels: Archangel Michael, Archangel Haniel

DAY 288

Channelled Angel message

You cannot awaken another.

Awakening is a sacred journey that activates at a divinely perfect moment.

Unity consciousness is acceptance of all others.

Your desire to awaken another creates separation and disunity.

Love, compassion and acceptance for both self and others dissolves all separation.

And so, rather than seek to change another, become the light that you wish to see in the world.

All is as it should be.

———— Invocation ————

Angels, please help me let go of my desire to change, control, or awaken another, and find unconditional acceptance for all beings now.

DAY 289

Channelled Angel message

Everything is a message.

Every feeling, emotion and experience offers you a pathway to a deeper understanding of your human experience.

When you slow down and still your mind, all the answers that you seek become clear in divine perfect timing. Often, discomfort is the trigger to inquiry that becomes clarity.

Learning to decode your own sacred vibrational heart messages is possible for everyone.

We can guide you. As can other sacred guides.

It's a process of unlearning. It's a process of listening and feeling.

Mostly, it's a process of trust.

Decoding your heart messages requires using a part of your beautiful, radiant mind/body/spirit system that you may be unfamiliar with initially. It may even feel scary to begin this journey, to break through collective programming or past-life experiences where intuition has been distorted or experienced as unsafe.

Intuition is a combination of inner curiosity, patience, love and faith.

You are a powerful and radiant being with untapped intuitive abilities. These are yours to claim just as you breathe and sleep.

In fact, you already use them without realising.

Messages are everywhere. It becomes easier and easier once you begin to seek and notice them.

Your heart is the key.

Does this *feel* like love? Does this *feel* like it's true for me? Does this *feel* like a message?

This journey is far simpler than it seems. And it's fun!

DAY 290

Channelled Angel message

Everything is shifting now.

If things feel dynamic, unsettled and fluid, that's because there is great change underway now.

All that you desire is birthing now.

In order for these changes to occur, you must surrender and let go of all that you are holding on to.

This is a body, mind, and spirit experience.

What beliefs are you holding on to?

What behaviours are you holding on to?

What relationships (with people, places, or structures) are you holding on to?

You are reaching a tremendous point of possibility, both individually and collectively (for both are connected: what occurs within then ripples without).

This transition period is asking everything of you, and the discomfort you are feeling is your consciousness shifting from the old to the new.

All that you knew to be safe and true is inverting now.

New perceptions, new understanding, new experiences, new relationships, new ideas, new energy. New reality. New Earth.

You are New Earth.

--- Invocation ---

I am the channel and conduit for the birth of the new reality. I am safe and held by my Angelic team as I shift in consciousness and embody that which I desire to see in the world.

Guiding Angels:
Archangel Metatron, Archangel Haniel, Archangel Michael

DAY 291

Channelled Angel message

You can change your reality. You are the magician.

Nothing is fixed. Everything is fluid. Magic is everywhere!

As you awaken and recall your magnificence, your awareness of your ability to change your reality begins to blossom.

This is a limitless experience.

Your capacity to hold light/love is limitless.

You are completely safe to envelop your body, mind, and spirit in light/love.

Your capacity to wield light/love is limitless. You are the creator. There is no other outside of yourself who has the power to change or create your reality. Only you.

You claim your power simply by realisation.

Waves of expansion into your heart and your light body occur as you are ready.

Light/love is safe.

Love/light heals all.

Light/love is accessible to you now as always.

The feeling of light/love is one you will recognise as a memory and feeling.

Love/light is enhanced in nature. It is enhanced in acts of love, kindness, and compassion. It is enhanced with faith and trust.

--------- Invocation ---------

Angels, please remind me that I am love/light, and that
I am the creator of my reality.

Guiding Angels:
Guardian Angels, Archangel Uriel, Archangel Ariel,
Archangel Jophiel

DAY 292

Channelled Angel message

At times, this shift will be uncomfortable, and this is to be expected. This experience is challenging all that you know to be true.

You are not alone in your experience. All are experiencing an inversion and shift in consciousness now.

You are not separate, and what occurs for one occurs for all, for the collective is made up of the sum of the individuals.

The collective consciousness and experience is but an outward reflection of the individual and inner experience.

If all that you see and understand seems to be topsy turvy and inside out, you are not alone.

The current experience is one of inversion. The collective process is both causing and reacting to the changes that you see. For this process is not linear but circular and dynamic and both cause and effect are true at once.

All that you understand to be true is now collapsing.

All that you believed possible is now limitless.

This may feel as if you do not have sure footing at times.

Mother Gaia is your footing. And the divine is your point of reference. For Mother Gaia is your touchpoint to remember all is well, and the support that you seek is available unconditionally in an instant.

You are a powerful beacon and magnifier of love! Indeed, you are the manifestation of miracles, and the only reminder you ever need of the divine!

When things feel unfamiliar, unsettling, or unusual, go to the earth to find your footing, and go within to find the love of the divine.

—————— Invocation ——————

Angels, please remind me that I have the unconditional support of Mother Gaia as I shift and change now.

Guiding Angels:
Archangel Gaia, Archangel Ariel, Archangel Gersisa

DAY 293

Channelled Angel message

It's ok to let go now. The divine will always guide you.

Whenever you feel blocked or stuck, this is always an opportunity to surrender and soften.

The current experience includes a great collective shift inward.

This shift is heart guided, and your own experience will be to discover all the ways that you have abandoned your inner heart and begin to trust yourself again.

Your heart is a powerful energetic magnet, attractor, and conductor.

Your heart will never lead you astray.

Your heart is asking you to soften, release control, and allow yourself to flow with the energy of the divine and all living beings.

This way has been taught to be dangerous, to be wrong.

The sovereign heart journey has been interrupted, severed, and hijacked.

The sovereign heart is able to heal and repair all.

Love heals all. Love is the way.

You will always know the way, and your heart will always guide you.

Your Angelic team is with you every step of the way, with love, acceptance, compassion, and whispered guidance.

———————— Invocation ————————

Angels, please help me take the first step to let go and trust my inner heart guidance now.

Guiding Angels:
Archangel Zadkiel, Archangel Chamuel, Archangel Raphael

DAY 294

Channelled Angel message

Clarity will come, but not how you expect. Let go and allow it to flow to you.

This time is one of great revelations.

Clarity always comes. When has it not?

This is a time of great insight, visions, and sudden understanding.

This is a time of many messages unexpectedly being delivered, as if in a flood.

This is a time of great awareness, and information being revealed.

You need not do anything.

Just be.

Give yourself space and time to receive and process this experience now.

This is a great shift.

─────── Invocation ───────

Angels, please help me let go of expectation so that I can be present to the gifts of clarity and revelations in this moment.

Guiding Angels: Archangel Faith, Archangel Haniel

DAY 295
Channelled Angel message

The way appears before you. You need not force it.

The path is always hidden. You are not meant to know how things will turn out. Glimpses are occasionally seen or felt, but even then, you have free will and can choose another pathway.

The way is energetic, and love/light is the energy.

You find the way by feeling your way forwards. It is as much an inwards journey as an outwards one (in fact, the outward ripples only occur in reaction to the inner experience).

Your heart has always been the key.

As you connect your heart to your mind now, your whole experience will invert and expand inwardly, infinitely.

This is the shift.

Your path may seem hidden now, but your ability to discover the next step was always with your grasp and within your heart.

Angels, please help me trust that I am exactly where I am meant to be, and to see the next step on my path.

Guiding Angels:
Archangel Faith, Guardian Angels, Archangel Chamuel

DAY 296

Channelled Angel message

The divine is found within.

The divine is love/light. It feels safe. It feels like home. It is expansive, accepting, calm and gentle.

The divine sees all of you because it is an aspect of you.

The divine is something you find within when you open your inner heart and reclaim your sovereign heart guidance.

This journey is both rebellious and private.

This journey is one of ongoing enquiry and curiosity.

This journey is a homecoming to self. A remembering.

We are here with you on this journey, but you are both the sacred guide and the welcoming arms.

Invocation

I am my teacher, my healer, my lover, my parent, and my friend.
I am the creator, and I am love.

Guiding Angels: All Angels

DAY 297

Channelled Angel message

Everything you understand to be fixed is changing now.

This is an exciting time for you, and for the collective.

An explosion of consciousness is beginning now.

It is birthed simultaneously through the individual and collective consciousness.

This explosion will result in exponential changes in your reality.

Changes in every area of the human experience will begin to birth now.

This is a time of great creation and change that will continue for many years.

You are part of this process. You chose to be here now.

As the birthing comes close, so does the ending and death. Death of beliefs, ideas, labels, structures, identities, thought forms, and all that is fixed. Nothing can avoid this change process, especially that which you assume is stable and permanent.

Be prepared and ready to see with new eyes that which you thought to be fixed and true. All is not as it seems. It is much better!

Revelations and clarity will be the catalyst to the death/rebirth.

Birth and death are cyclical and connected.

You are safe and this is a wondrous experience.

 Invocation ——————

Angels, please help me find peace through a time of great destruction, death, and birth.

Guiding Angels:
Archangel Azrael, Archangel Nathaniel, Archangel Chamuel

DAY 298

Channelled Angel message

Intuition increases as your love increases.

Intuition is your energetic heart frequency interacting with the energy of other people, places, times, events and dimensions.

Nothing is impossible. All that you can imagine can be created with the energy of love.

Your precognitive sensations are your energetic interaction with future/now experiences.

To develop your intuition, all you need to do is develop your capacity to love.

Love opens your heart. Love heals. Love connects you with the divine. Love manifests and creates. Love is the frequency of creation, and of the divine.

You are safe to surrender to your inner heart wisdom, to your inner sovereign knowing.

You are safe to love.

———— Invocation ————

Angels, please help me feel safe on the journey of opening to love and to my own powerful intuition.

Guiding Angels:
Archangel Chamuel, Archangel Haniel, Archangel Michael

DAY 299

Channelled Angel message

You are safe to express your unique gifts.

You are safe to be you.

You are safe to claim all your power.

You are safe to think your thoughts and opinions.

You are safe to do the things you love, to live the way you feel guided.

You need not seek approval or permission. You need no validation.

Your energy will radiate vitality when you realise that it is only for you that you live.

Does this action feel heart guided for you? Then it is your truth to be actioned or expressed.

Energy flows when you lovingly allow it and express it. Fear contracts energy and stunts its flow.

There is nothing to fear. You are both safe and powerful.

—————— Invocation ——————

Angels, please help me gently open to feel safe expressing all parts of myself.

Guiding Angels:
Archangel Nathaniel, Archangel Jophiel, Archangel Michael

DAY 300

Channelled Angel message

Everything you seek outside yourself is found inside.

You are your teacher, your healer, your lover, your parent, your child.

And all that you seek is found at the exact right time, with a shift in awareness.

You see when you are ready.

You learn when you are ready.

You receive when you are ready.

You heal when you are ready.

For it happens this way, so how could it not be so?

And so, rather than fight and push and control, we ask you to notice and investigate and soften.

Self-enquiry will transform your world.

No other is better than, more qualified, more experienced, more expert.

No other is coming to rescue or love you.

And as you know that you integrate with the one and only. You.

It was always you. There is no other.

All you experience is an aspect of you, a mirror with which to understand yourself and find peace within.

A gentler way of being exists. Peace with yourself exists. Whole self-expression exists.

The journey is the point, and all is perfectly divine, for you also chose the journey.

──────── Invocation ────────

Angels, please help me become, embody, and
express all that I seek.

Guiding Angels: Archangel Nathaniel, Guardian Angels

DAY 301

Channelled Angel message

A softer, easier way is coming. How can you allow that to birth through you now?

The beginnings of a rebirth are seeding now.

This experience will feel new to you and is birthing through your consciousness.

You are currently being shown every way that no longer works. Old ways. Old ideas. Old beliefs. Old responses.

The challenge is to find a new way.

The new way is vulnerable, soft, and heart led.

The new way at times will feel risky and unfamiliar.

The new way feels blind.

The new way is a feeling way, without rules, without guidance, without experts, without governance, without sacrifice.

The new way is chosen and embodied.

The new way is of the sovereign heart.

The new way is inwards, private, and sacred.

The new way requires every human to rebel into their sacred heart awakening and become all aspects of their full authentic expression.

The new way is the return of the divine organic human blueprint.

——————— Invocation ———————

The heart awakening occurring within me now is a sacred path that I chose to walk. I chose to be here now for this very journey.

Guiding Angels:
Archangel Haniel, Archangel Chamuel, Archangel Faith

DAY 302

Channelled Angel message

New Earth is birthing now. The process is a divine process of magic. What you imagine now, births now.

Your imagination is that which connects you to the divine, and to the energy of love/light.

Your imagination is that which channels and receives

guidance.

Your imagination is that which manifests and creates.

Your imagination is your divination tool, your magic wand, and your connection to us.

As a new world is created, it is imagined, for both are linked and there is no beginning or end point. Only now.

Allow yourself to feel all that you desire to be, all that you desire to see, into form.

Imagination and feeling are the key.

Heart and mind.

———— Invocation ————

Angels, please remind me that my imagination and love are the key to the birth of this new reality. I am the conduit and the creator.

Guiding Angels:
Archangel Ariel, Archangel Haniel, Archangel Metatron

DAY 303

Channelled Angel message

Your heart always knows what it needs.

It is time now for the sacred heart awakening.

This journey is being experienced by both the individual and the collective (for both are linked and are one).

The journey of the sacred heart awakening is within, is compassionate, is forgiving, and is a whispered journey of reconnection to your inner heart.

All that you seek is found within, with the gentle and loving guidance of your own sacred heart.

No other will ever have the answers. They merely guide and

witness your own remembering of your sovereign truth.

Your heart will always guide you true. The journey now is to begin to ask your heart, rather than seek the answers outside or from another.

You are ready. You are your sacred heart guide now.

——————— Invocation ———————

Angels, please remind me that the answers I seek will be found through listening to my own heart guidance.

Guiding Angels:
Archangel Chamuel, Archangel Haniel, Archangel Faith

DAY 304

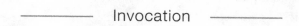

Your connection with the divine can always be rekindled.

There is never a reason for us to abandon you or give up on you.

We are always with you.

We are always accepting of every choice you make.

We love you infinitely in every moment of your life.

Whether you are aware or not, we (and therefore the divine) are always with you and always love you.

Remembering your connection to us (and therefore the divine) happens at the exact right moment in the exact right way.

We love you until then, and always.

Remembering your relationship with us (and the divine) is heart led, and faith led.

Remembering your connection to the divine is a blind leap of faith.

Remembering your connection to the divine is activated in

your own heart.

Love awakens this journey.

Love guides you, and your sacred sovereign heart knows the way.

Deciphering your heart messages and our whispers is sacred, private and unique to you.

A sacred guide can assist you.

─────── Invocation ───────

Angels, please remind me that I am safe to begin to trust the whispers and signs from my Angelic team and open my heart to a deeper relationship with the divine now.

Guiding Angels:
Archangel Uriel, Archangel Chamuel, Archangel Michael

DAY 305

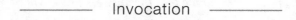
Channelled Angel message

Your truth will always emerge if you listen to your heart.

Remembering your sacred heart language can feel confusing at times.

The journey asks you to do things differently, in a way that will feel unfamiliar and new.

A sacred guide can assist you.

Choose someone who empowers you to look for answers within.

We can assist you. Ask us for help when you feel lost, when the path escapes you, when you can't feel or see the answers.

The secret is asking your heart and allowing space to hear the whispered answers.

Your heart speaks the language of feelings. Of love.

Learning to decode this language is a process of patience, compassion, allowing and accepting.

To make this feel easier, spend time in nature. Disconnect from technology. Create a quiet space around you. And practise writing about your feelings.

Your truth will always emerge when given space for expression.

——————— Invocation ———————

Angels, please remind me that learning my sacred heart language takes time and patience.

Guiding Angels:
Archangel Chamuel, Archangel Zadkiel, Archangel Faith

DAY 306

Channelled Angel message

Your path now is to be all that you love.

This was all you ever needed to do. But now that you know, you can focus your heart and choices on this pathway.

What do you love?

What brings joy into your heart?

What feels good to explore (even if it doesn't seem to make sense to others)?

What would you never regret learning, teaching, exploring, expressing, creating?

What brings a smile to your face as you imagine it?

What softens your heart as you feel the energy of the experience?

This is the secret to manifesting and also to intuition.

This is the secret to self-expression and finding your purpose.

Love. It's all about love.

Invocation

Angels, please help me begin to live my life from a place of heart guidance, and love.

Guiding Angels:
Archangel Chamuel, Archangel Zadkiel, Archangel Faith

DAY 307

Channelled Angel message

Hold steady and trust your heart vision. All is unfolding as it should.

Transition periods feel uncomfortable. There is a palpable mix of both creation and destruction energy in transitions.

Old patterns, relationships, and contracts end.

New habits, relationships, ideas, and pathways form.

All occur at once.

This is a time when multiple timelines exist in a fluid state at once.

You can do nothing to force change in this situation. It will anchor and shift at the exact divinely perfect moment.

All you need do is hold resonance with your heart vision and let that feeling blossom and expand to envelop you in faith.

Faith in yourself. Faith in your truth. Faith in your story, your future, and your intuition.

All is unfolding exactly as it should.

Invocation

Angels, when my situation feels uncomfortable and in flux, please help me let go and trust that all is as it should be so that I can open to receive miracles.

DAY 308

Channelled Angel message

All you ever need to do is see how the energy feels. There is your answer.

Your heart can tune into the frequency of any person, situation, or event.

Your heart will give you a reading based on the energy of that person, situation, or event.

You can practise this exercise and become competent and then confident decoding the messages of the heart.

Energy is truth. You are a powerful energetic being. Energy never lies.

Energy has no boundaries of space or time.

Energy crosses oceans instantly. Energy is multidimensional. Energy connects you to future/past versions of self and others.

It's instant and it's full knowing.

Love is your frequency, your current, your signal.

——————— Invocation ———————

Angels, please remind me that learning to feel the language and frequency of love is my highest priority now.

Guiding Angels: Archangel Chamuel, Archangel Faith

DAY 309

Channelled Angel message

You can change how an experience feels instantly. Peace is always available.

Everything happens for a reason. You rarely understand the spiritual purpose of an experience until after the energy has shifted. You are not meant to know why something is happening as it happens, and you are not meant to know how it will turn out.

This offers a pathway for peace.

How can you look at your current experience with new eyes?

We can assist you through this journey.

Some questions you can ask us are:

- *What am I missing in this experience?*
- *What is my highest priority here?*
- *How can I approach this differently?*
- *What messages do you have for me to assist me through this challenge?*

We will always guide you. We are always with you. Things will always shift, and there is always peace to be found.

Things are not as they seem. They are much, much better.

———— Invocation ————

Angels, please help me let go of all attachment, resistance, and control so that I can open to the experience I am having right now in this moment.

Guiding Angels: Archangel Faith, Archangel Haniel

DAY 310

Channelled Angel message

Curiosity is the pathway to rediscovering your sacred heart wisdom.

Your heart unfolds gently.

You are safe to ask your heart what it needs, and what you need.

Your heart will guide you at the exact right pace to let down its walls, and open to an energetic circuit connection with source and all living beings.

This process is already underway for you and all.

Love is the new way. Love is guiding the birth of a new experience for you, and for the collective.

Gently explore your life with playful curiosity now.

This need not be a serious or difficult journey. Love is indeed joyful, healing, accepting and compassionate, after all.

——————— Invocation ———————

Angels, please remind me that the path to love is one filled with miracles, and that I need not fear this journey.

Guiding Angels: Archangel Chamuel, Archangel Michael

DAY 311

Channelled Angel message

Everything is not as it seems. It is much better.

Reality, and consciousness, is in the process of an inversion and shift.

Up until now, there has been one operating reality.

Now there are two.

One operating reality is still connected to the old paradigm. The other operating reality is beginning to see with a new filter and receive and anchor a unity experience.

As the split occurs, it will seem as if all is getting worse in the world.

We assure you; this is not the case.

Things appear to be one way. In fact, they are another.

The old paradigm says *Be afraid*.

The new world reconnects all to love and oneness.

This shift is underway now. All will be well.

Change appears to be difficult.

Change is what births a new world.

———————— Invocation ————————

Angels, please hold me steady through this time of tremendous upheaval and change, so that I can hold the vision for a new earth reality now.

Guiding Angels:
Archangel Nathaniel, Archangel Azrael, Archangel Michael

DAY 312

Channelled Angel message

The shift in consciousness is inwards, with a return to heart sovereignty.

You do not need to 'do' anything. All is as it should be.

This journey is occurring for one and all.

Each heart awakens to the divine at the exact right moment.

As the new light codes anchor now, a mass inner heart awakening is underway.

All will look within when all outside no longer makes sense.

Until that moment, the sovereign will be the expert, government, doctor, teacher, scientist or other authority.

Only when all these 'officials' no longer make sense will the individual look within for the answers.

And then each soul will find love, the divine and a new experience of consciousness that requires no sovereign, other than self.

The return to sovereign self is both the hardest and the easiest journey the collective will make.

It seems impossible, and yet it will be so simple.

A paradox that perfectly fits the experience of the reunification of heart and mind.

The split occurring now will seem insurmountable. And yet, polarity will create unity when the inversion point is reached by the collective consciousness.

Hold steady and soften inwards now.

——————— Invocation ———————

Angels, please remind me that even though this shift seems impossible, I am experiencing it anyway. There is nothing I cannot handle, and I am experiencing a miracle.

Guiding Angels: Archangel Uriel, Archangel Metatron

DAY 313

Channelled Angel message

When the pathway does not seem clear, it is found within.

It can take time to begin to listen to the whispers of your heart.

It is easier to look for solutions, make decisions, push through, take action, ask for advice and follow the crowd.

Even still, sometimes the pathway is unclear, and you will feel confused, uncertain, or blocked.

When all outside no longer makes sense, the answer is found within.

This is the moment of awakening. This is the surrender point when the heart reconnects with the divine.

Faith is found in the heart. Sovereignty is reclaimed in the heart.

It is ok to not know the way. In fact, this is to be celebrated. Your journey to self begins the moment you realise that the outside world does not satisfy you.

This is the inversion point.

The return to sovereign heart self is the inversion of consciousness playing out in the collective now.

As you experience confusion, blindness, or disillusionment without, you will awaken your heart guidance within.

This is a sacred journey, and you are guided and supported every step of the way by your personal Guardian Angels.

——————— Invocation ———————

Angels, please help me let go and fall inwards to my inner heart now, knowing I am safe and held by the divine in this leap of faith.

Guiding Angels: Guardian Angels, Archangel Faith

DAY 314

Channelled Angel message

Invert everything you know to be true.

All that seemed solid is now in flux. All that was true is not.

The shift is an inversion of consciousness.

The current operating reality is from an outdated filter or

perspective.

What you see is not congruent with what you feel.

This is a result of the heart-mind split. A distortion and split that occurred in stages thousands of years ago.

The heart-mind split is healing now. This reconnection of heart and mind will create a new experience of reality. Where heart and mind were once separate, they are now becoming one, and feeling and thought will unify the division/polarity/separation/split.

As you feel your way forwards, all that you once understood from a mind perspective will require you to feel from a heart perspective.

Intuition will explode. Love and connection will explode. Unity will be possible because it is felt by all.

And so, as you begin this journey, become curious.

What is this belief/experience? What does my mind tell me? What does my heart feel? What do I see/feel with my senses?

This is the awakening.

––––––– Invocation –––––––

Angels, please help me let go and journey my heart awakening without force or resistance.

Guiding Angels:
Archangel Haniel, Archangel Metatron, Archangel Faith

DAY 315

Channelled Angel message

Uncertainty is a message waiting to come through. Hold steady and trust your vision.

It feels unfamiliar initially using your intuition and your heart guidance.

We want to assist you.

Clarity always comes.

When you know that change is coming, this is a part of the intuitive process.

Ideas and inspiration are a precognitive energy transmission of a future/now version of yourself.

You are receiving a transmission to assist you on the process from here to there.

Intuitive messages are emotions and energy as well as visions and knowing.

When you receive an inspired vision, ask yourself, how does this message feel? Does it feel good? Is it something that you would like to experience?

If so, then allow. Trust. Become. Emerge. Blossom.

You need not force the process. In fact, you cannot.

Uncertainty is something you can alchemise, once you remember that it is a part of the process.

All will become clear at the exact divine perfect moment.

If it is not clear, then it is not the right moment.

We will not tell you when or how things will play out. That would violate your free will.

We will help you find peace in the journey and see your next steps. Is this not a more empowering experience anyway?

———————— Invocation ————————

Angels, please help me find peace and patience now as I let go and trust that the clarity I desire will come.

Guiding Angels:
Archangel Nathaniel, Archangel Faith, Archangel Haniel

DAY 316

Channelled Angel message

Truth is not absolute. Your heart whispers your truth.

Your truth does not lie outside of yourself.

Another does not determine your truth, regardless of their expertise.

Your heart will always send you messages to help you find your way.

Beginning to listen to your heart can feel confusing. Is this my heart wisdom? Or is this fear/ego?

Your heart language is one of love, not of fear.

Your ego speaks with fear, caution, anger and shame.

Your heart speaks with acceptance, with compassion, with passion, with humour, with joy.

Your heart sends emotional pulses and energetic sensations through your physical body to help you decode the truth of a situation.

Energy never lies. And your heart knows you and your needs better than any other.

We also speak to you via energy that you can feel in your heart.

When you are looking for your pathway, and seeking your truth, ask your heart, and ask us to assist you with clear messages that you can easily feel, see, and hear.

This is the journey of reclaiming and reawakening your sovereign heart wisdom.

———————— Invocation ————————

Angels, please help me trust my heart now.

Guiding Angels: Archangel Chamuel, Archangel Faith

DAY 317

Channelled Angel message

Opening your heart to the divine will help you feel safe, connected, and loved.

We notice a belief that you might become vulnerable, at risk or unsafe opening your energy and heart to the divine.

We want to say that the opposite is true.

By keeping your heart closed, protected, and disconnected from the divine, you are also keeping yourself closed, disconnected, and protected from all living beings.

Your experience of life is then filtered.

You will experience love and connection on a minuscule level compared to what is available to you in your open-hearted state.

The shift occurring now asks you to open your heart and awaken to your glorious, radiant, fully connected divine state.

Your intuition will increase as you connect energetically with the energy circuits of all life.

You will experience greater empathy, heightened intuitive awareness and a stronger sense of self.

As you open your heart, it will feel unfamiliar and new at first, however, this will settle.

You will then notice that life seems miraculous! Joyful! Filled with blissful love!

You will receive empathic and intuitive messages from all living beings, and from the divine (as well as—of course—from us, your Angelic team).

It will soon feel like home.

It is your home.

This is your natural state, and when you make this shift, you will forever feel calmer, more peaceful, less anxious, more loving. For you will feel your oneness, and our love!

You are safe to open your heart.

Angels, please help me feel safe opening to my inner heart awakening now.

Guiding Angels:
Archangel Michael, Archangel Chamuel, Archangel Haniel

DAY 318

Channelled Angel message

All that you seek can be found quickly by doing the exact opposite to that which you have been taught.

Life can be easy.

You can heal quickly.

There is abundance for everyone.

You have powerful intuition.

Every situation that feels challenging can be experienced with love, grace, and miracles.

All that you need to do is choose the exact opposite pathway to that which you have been taught.

Have you been taught to follow orders? Don't. Follow your heart.

Have you been taught to listen to experts? Don't. Listen to your own intuition and powerful reason.

Have you been taught what is fact and fiction by authorities? Question everything and research for yourself.

Have you been taught to be busy and work hard? There is no need. You can find abundance with peace, balance, and full soul expression.

Apply this simple process to every challenge you might face.

What is truth? Question everything now. Invert your own thought process and you will discover a new reality that is available to you now. This new expression is loving, accepting, gentle, connected, intuitive and respectful of individual heart sovereignty.

Heart sovereignty is returning to the collective now.

This awakening will be the most significant of your life.

<hr/>

Invocation

Angels, please help me trust my own judgement,
intuition, and reason now.

Guiding Angels:
Archangel Jophiel, Archangel Haniel, Archangel Michael

DAY 319

Channelled Angel message

To find your sovereign heart wisdom, clear your mind and energy of noise.

The busier you are, the harder it will seem to hear and feel your sovereign truth, and also our guidance.

There are many things that create noise in your physical and energetic body.

Physical clutter, an overloaded schedule, and noise from outside sources such as TV, internet and radio, all create an experience of 'too much noise' and an inability to tune in to your inner whispered wisdom.

This is exacerbated by a weakened physical state caused by toxins in food, water, and the environment.

This constant 'too much' noise makes it almost impossible to hear your heart and your intuition.

However, this is very easily remedied.

Declutter and cleanse your space and your energy.

You need only make one small step at a time. Start by taking half an hour in nature each day, with no disturbances or distractions.

And go slowly, one step at a time from there to create space in your physical home/schedule and also your energetic field.

This will create powerful changes for you immediately!

——————— Invocation ———————

Angels, please help me through the process of a physical and energetic detox, so that I can remove all that is creating noise and distraction from my field and my life.

Guiding Angels:
Archangel Jophiel, Archangel Jeremiel,
Archangel Michael, Archangel Raphael

DAY 320

Channelled Angel message

Your purpose is everything that is experienced on the journey from here to there.

The journey is the point. It is always about here, now, and never about there or when.

Yes, indeed this means there is very little for you to do. In fact, if the purpose is the experience, how might your 'now' experience change with this knowledge?

How might you soften your pace, and flow with your current experience?

If the experience is the point, does it then follow that every single moment has meaning? That everything is a gift and miracle? Yes indeed!

And so, does it not also indicate that everything is a message, and everything happens for a reason to assist you on your journey?

And so, rather than fight to change your situation, we invite you to embrace it. For it is perfect. It will change exactly when it's meant to. And that normally happens faster when you soften into experiencing the journey right now. For all that you are meant to experience suddenly becomes clear to you once you look around you and embrace this moment.

—————— Invocation ——————

Angels, please help me let go of the destination and embrace the experience I am having right now in this moment. For it is perfect.

Guiding Angels: Archangel Michael, Archangel Faith

DAY 321

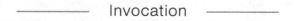
Channelled Angel message

Ask and you will be shown.

We will never violate your free will.

We will never tell you your future or show you the outcome.

However, with your permission, we can show you the next step, and reveal that which you cannot see but is right before your eyes.

There is always a next step.

There is always a message available to you that will assist you right now in this moment.

Look left and right. Look within. Look right in front of you, and there you will find the answers you seek.

Take your focus away from the outcome, and the future.

We will show you what is right here in front of your eyes. This is the answer that you need (if not the answer to the question that you believe you need answered).

Working with us will always give you clarity. Not always in the way you want. Always for your highest good, and always respecting your free will.

──────────── Invocation ────────────

Angels, please show me what I can't see. Please help me find the next step on my path.

Guiding Angels:
Archangel Haniel, Archangel Michael, Archangel Faith

DAY 322

Channelled Angel message

Learning to see through the veil takes practice. Trust your vision.

As the veil lifts now, you are experiencing a new vision of self, and a new vision of the world.

At times, this might feel confusing, as you will question all that you understood to be true.

Up until now, your mind has been your guide. You have experienced a thinking reality that has been externally validated.

Your experience has been created by external sources for education, teaching and validation.

This is inverting now.

Your heart is now your guide.

As the veil lifts, your heart awakens to your full sovereign power.

You remember and realise that you are your teacher, your healer, your guru and your guide.

This can feel at times like you are switching between two different realities. Indeed, you are.

Give yourself time to learn/remember your sacred heart wisdom. For it exists within and cannot be learned from another.

This language is subtle, nuanced, gentle, compassionate, and whispered.

It requires patience, faith, and love to learn.

Your vision, feelings and messages will become stronger and clearer with time and practice.

We will support you.

———————— Invocation ————————

Angels, please help me trust my own powerful reason, logic, intuition, feelings, and wisdom.

Guiding Angels:
Guardian Angels, Archangel Haniel, Archangel Michael

DAY 323

Channelled Angel message

When joy, love and curiosity are your guide, there are no mistakes.

Remember that you chose to be here now.

Remember that you chose to explore the full spectrum of the human experience.

And so, if you live with fear as your guide, you will miss opportunities and experience life from a contracted frequency.

If you open to the constant flow and support of the divine, and let curiosity, love and joy guide you, life will blossom, expand, and open all around you.

It will seem as if there are no mistakes, for you will not feel attached to your experiences.

Joy, love and curiosity break the spell of attachment, and of fear.

They bring you into your sovereign truth and disconnect you from the collective consciousness.

You find your way when you let go and live from a place of wonder, with the divine as your ever-present energetic support.

—————— Invocation ——————

Angels, please help me break the spell of attachment and fear and live from a place of curiosity and love.

Guiding Angels:
Archangel Michael, Archangel Jophiel, Archangel Chamuel

DAY 324

Channelled Angel message

Everything shifts when you reconnect with the divine.

What is the divine? The divine is infinite love. It exists for you to access in any given moment.

It is that which creates life. It is that which you feel as love, joy and bliss in your heart.

It is expressed as form all around you.

You are indeed not separate from the divine, other than in your perception of separation.

As soon as you recall your oneness, and your natural right to flow with the constant energy of love, everything shifts.

Your experience inverts and you see things with a completely different perspective.

Fear dissolves.

You recall and remember your radiance, your brilliance, your ability to heal and to create miracles instantly, and your innate worth.

This process is an inner awakening, and it is occurring now on a mass-consciousness level.

You are safe to recall your connection to love. To us. To all living beings. To the divine as you understand it.

And to your own sacred sovereign heart.

———————— Invocation ————————

*Angels, please help me let go of all fear and open to
a relationship with the divine now.*

Guiding Angels: Archangel Michael, Archangel Uriel

DAY 325

Channelled Angel message

Become curious about any message that claims authority over you.

You are a powerful sovereign being. A living miracle connected to the infinite divine love of source, and all living beings.

No other knows your truth. No other is an expert over you.

Every single experience can be observed from a position of personal power.

Interaction with all others outside of yourself can be navigated from a curious exploration of your own sovereignty.

Wisdom is found in all interactions. You chose to explore this human experience in relationship to others. This is part of the miracle of learning about love.

You do not need to give your power away to any other on this journey.

You are not required to be the same. To have the same opinion. To make the same choices.

The inversion of consciousness occurring now is a collective reclamation of personal sovereign power.

As you navigate your own inversion of consciousness, this can be explored with detachment, faith, and curiosity.

Does this person/organisation/label or identity require me to give up personal freedom? Do they/does it require me to abandon my beliefs, my health, or my sovereignty in any way?

What is true for another may not be true for you. That is the miraculous magic of the human experience, and very soon this will become the majority experience in the collective.

Until then, we invite you to be curious and explore your reality.

--------- Invocation ---------

Angels, please help me be curious and discerning with all external guidance that asserts authority over me. Please help me set strong boundaries and trust my own inner wisdom.

Guiding Angels: Archangel Michael

DAY 326

Channelled Angel message

You have potential that you cannot yet fathom.

Your ability to create, manifest, heal, love, and see is not yet fully realised. In fact, you have barely scratched the surface.

There is no description we are able to give you that fully encapsulates the coming shift. For the new reality does not yet exist in a way that can be understood.

You will birth this journey, individually and collectively.

This is your purpose. To co-create and birth a new era of consciousness.

And so, you need not understand. You need not define. All

you need do is be curious, open, and trusting of your sacred and powerful relationship with the divine.

We remind you: the divine is love.

You are love. You are the divine expressed as form. Realisation of your magnificence is the gateway to expression of your full potential.

——————— Invocation ———————

Angels, please help me let go of all attachment to disclosure, revelations and change now so that I can be present for the experience of birthing the new reality.

Guiding Angels:
Archangel Faith, Archangel Haniel, Archangel Metatron

DAY 327

Channelled Angel message

You are powerful. No other has power over you.

Power is energy. It is your life force, your vitality, your imagination, and intuition.

Power is the energy of love/light; the energy that creates all, and connects all.

You are innately powerful, just as you are innately worthy, enough, and loveable, simply by your existence.

Any message or person that claims power over you can be rejected instantly by your realisation that your power cannot be taken by another.

As the collective consciousness shifts now, a reclamation of power is occurring.

This shift is one of awareness.

It is a return to heart sovereignty, experienced simply by

realisation.

It is both simple and complex.

It is both easy and difficult.

The moment you understand, it occurs, and all charge dissipates.

The extent of your fully embodied power is beyond your comprehension.

You are safe to reclaim your full power now.

──────── Invocation ────────

Angels, please help me experience a quantum leap and realise that I am powerful, sovereign, and free.

Guiding Angels: Archangel Michael, Archangel Metatron

DAY 328

Channelled Angel message

Until now, your programming has been external.

Your experience has been created by your external reality. By identities, labels, information received and processed, by experts, teachers and by authorities outside of yourself.

Your independence, emotionality, intuition, and power have been stunted and restricted as a result.

Full soul expression has not been realised but by a few who were able to invert the current reality and find enlightenment.

Now the collective is experiencing a consciousness shift so great, that a mass inner heart awakening is occurring.

Over dozens of years, this shift has been occurring, with a peak inversion point (which is in fact a series of inversion points) now imminent.

Reality is shifting from an external, thinking, authority-based perception, to an internal, feeling, individual sovereign perception.

The result will be an explosion of love.

An explosion of consciousness.

A flashbang inversion point where love becomes the dominant energetic frequency, and fear begins to recede and dissolve.

The veil is an energetic manifestation woven with fear, control, and deception.

Love breaks through the veil. Awareness breaks through the veil.

All programming held with the old coding is collapsing now.

Love/light is expanding exponentially.

You are safe to open your heart to experience this new reality birthing now, through you.

—————— Invocation ——————

Angels, please help me remember that I chose to be here now for this experience. As all changes around me, please remind me that I am safe, and my purpose is to experience this shift.

Guiding Angels:
Archangel Nathaniel, Archangel Michael, Archangel Faith

DAY 329

Channelled Angel message

As the vibration rises now, all that was created from fear will be exposed.

This is a time of great change and revelations.

The light/love frequency has risen to a point where it is now expanding exponentially.

The immediate first result will be that all that was hidden

becomes visible.

This will occur both for the individual and for the collective.

The revelations will begin and continue, for your understanding of yourself, and for your perception of the world.

This can be an uncomfortable process. To witness your own shadows is painful at times. And it is also necessary. Light and darkness are both a part of the human experience. They are being integrated now.

This is why the most important thing you can do now is continue to focus on your self-healing and expressing your light and your love.

All you need to do is focus on love. Love will guide you and the collective through this process now.

Have faith and hold steady.

——————— Invocation ———————

Angels, please remind me that I am safe, that I am not alone, and that I chose to be here now for this experience.

Guiding Angels:
Archangel Michael, Archangel Faith, Archangel Uriel

DAY 330

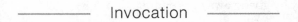

Channelled Angel message

Ask for a sign now, and what you most need will be revealed.

We are always available to assist you.

We have your highest good in mind at all times, and will never violate your free will, or the free will of another.

We can always offer guidance, love, and support. However, what you most need may not look like what you most want.

And so, we assure you that our answers, our signs, and our guidance will always be that which you most need to see or hear.

And so, we ask you to let go of attachment to a specific outcome, or a specific result.

As you begin to work more closely with us, we invite you to take a leap of faith.

The outcome that is perfect for you will eventuate at the exact right moment.

Trust the process. Allow yourself to soften now. See the signs and messages we offer you now, as they will assist you in the way you most need, right here and right now in this moment on your journey.

We offer you guidance to the peace that you seek, and clues to the path that you cannot see.

We will never rob you of the miraculous experience of your journey by giving away the ending.

The experience, the learning, the growth, and the miracles are far more valuable than finding out the outcome.

Let go, embrace the unknown, and invite our love in to support you on your journey.

―――――― Invocation ――――――

Angels, please help me find peace with the unknown and miraculous aspect of my human experience. Please help me open to a deeper relationship with you along the way.

Guiding Angels:
Archangel Faith, Guardian Angels, Archangel Uriel

DAY 331

Channelled Angel message

Divine timing is neither fast nor slow. It is perfect.

Everything happens at the exact right moment.

There are no errors.

You have no control over the timing of that which you desire.

Control will not bring that which you desire to you any faster. In fact, it will do the exact opposite.

The moment when something occurs is perfect because of every single moment that has led to that moment!

And it is perfect because of all the experiences and lessons, for all people involved.

Surrender and faith create a pathway to that which you desire.

Gratitude for all you have in this moment creates a pathway to that which you desire.

Curious exploration of the journey accelerates the frequency journey to that which you desire, when explored with detachment.

When you explore your desires from this perspective, time becomes irrelevant.

Each moment becomes a wondrous exploration of the full spectrum of the human experience.

Remember, you were born at the exact divinely perfect moment. How could every other occurrence not be a manifestation of the same perfect divine timing?

----------- Invocation -----------

Angels, please help me let go of all attachment and control to embrace my life exactly as it is in this moment.

Guiding Angels: Archangel Michael, Archangel Faith

DAY 332

Channelled Angel message

Love is the energy of creation, of manifesting, of healing and of intuition.

Love is the energy of the divine.

Love is all you ever need to guide you in all decisions and situations.

Love is literally able to create form from nothing.

And so, we gift you the biggest secret now …

You are the creator, and you create with love.

And as you realise this, you collectively shift from a reason- and thinking-based reality, to a feeling- and love-based reality.

This is the shift occurring now.

The age of love is anchoring now, as realised by your own awareness and shift.

——— Invocation ———

I am the creator. I am love. I am safe to love,
dream, imagine and feel.

Guiding Angels:
Archangel Chamuel, Archangel Ariel, Archangel Metatron

DAY 333

Channelled Angel message

As there is no time, there is also no rush. Time is not running out. You exist infinitely.

This unlearning will at times feel as if you are experiencing a glitch. For all you have been taught says the opposite … almost as if it's been programmed.

'Time is running out.'

'You only live once.'

'There are not enough hours in the day.'

And so, we invite you to remember that you are indeed an infinite being of universal consciousness born from the same energy that creates stars.

We invite you to remember that you are made from the energy of pure divine love.

We invite you to remember that you are consciousness expressed as form, a miracle.

You do not end. You are infinite.

You exist consciously beyond this lifetime that you are experiencing now. You have had many lives previously and will have many more until you ascend to the higher light dimensions.

And so, you may let go now.

There is no rush. All is exactly as it should be. You are here, right now, and that is all you ever need be.

In this moment, where is the love?

For every situation, should you ask this question—and allow your radiant, powerful heart to explore this as an energy and feeling—you will become and magnetise all that you desire.

It is time now to unlock from the attachment to time.

──────── Invocation ────────

Angels, please help me identify and let go of all outdated beliefs about time, so that I can become an infinite expression of the divine in this moment, and flow peacefully with my experience.

Guiding Angels: Archangel Michael

DAY 334

Channelled Angel message

Your heart is far more powerful than you realise.

Your heart is an energetic conductor that transmits and receives energy—the energy of the divine, the energy of all creation, the energy of love.

Your heart is able to give you signals to help you navigate your experience, by way of feelings and emotions.

When expressed fully, your heart is a powerful creator, and when combined with your imagination, your heart can manifest all that you desire.

Your heart speaks the language of frequency. Of love.

Full expression of your powerful heart leads to full expression of your powerful self.

Your heart can guide you to an answer for every question you have, and you can learn its subtle and nuanced language.

We speak to you through your heart.

Your higher self speaks to you through your heart.

Your ancestors speak to you through your heart.

And so, as you experience a shift now, we invite you to open your heart and surrender to letting go.

The thinking reality is dismantling.

The feeling reality is birthing.

Trust your heart now.

─────── Invocation ───────

Angels, please help me let go in this moment so that I can be present to my experience of love.

Guiding Angels:
Archangel Faith, Archangel Michael, Archangel Metatron

DAY 335

Channelled Angel message

The shift you are experiencing is like operating from a new software system. The new software is love.

As you shift now, at times you will feel like nothing makes sense. The old reality no longer applies. The new reality has not anchored.

This shift in consciousness is not external, it is internal, heart based, and embodied and birthed through you.

Each individual has a role to play now.

The heart chakra of each individual is activating to receive and transmit divine sovereign love now.

This is a faith journey, with no external guide.

This is a love journey, with love now your guiding light.

Does this feel like love?

That is your most important question now.

--------- Invocation ---------

Angels, please help me see clearly all that feels like love to me.

Guiding Angels:
Archangel Haniel, Archangel Metatron, Archangel Chamuel

DAY 336

Channelled Angel message

Everything you desire comes exactly when you realise you are ready.

It is all an inward journey.

No action is required unless it is heart guided and for love.

You create with your heart, with your consciousness, with your mind in circuitry with your powerful energy.

Your desires are created within and are attracted to you via your frequency.

The frequency is love.

The most powerful thing you can do is explore love. Love of self, and love of others, in all ways.

Truthfully, this is your only purpose. It is the reason you chose to incarnate here, now.

And so, all the secrets that you need to navigate this journey are quite simple.

Explore love in all ways, and all will be well.

———————— Invocation ————————

Angels, please help me refocus my attention to love now.

Guiding Angels: Archangel Chamuel

DAY 337

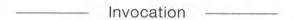
Channelled Angel message

Trust and faith are found within.

The journey of reclaiming your sovereignty is internal, via your heart.

It is private, sacred, and unique for each individual.

Every human is experiencing an inner heart awakening now.

Whilst there are many sacred guides on this journey, it is travelled alone, and within.

The voice is yours alone to trust.

The feelings are yours alone to interpret.

The surrender moment is faced alone.

The blind faith required cannot be taught and is discovered

within.

Trust is not bestowed by another. There is no authority, divine or otherwise.

Trust is found within, after the surrender moment is reached.

And then it is journeyed again, and again and again, as you deepen into your magnificent, radiant, powerful heart.

Let go now.

The trust and faith you seek are right there, within your own heart.

——————— Invocation ———————

Angels, please help me walk this knife's edge towards surrender, faith, and trust. Please help me have the strength and courage to let go when it is time.

Guiding Angels: Archangel Faith, Archangel Haniel

DAY 338

Channelled Angel message

Everything that feels difficult now is part of the solution.

Everything happens for a reason.

Delays, obstacles, and challenges all have a purpose.

Curiously explore your current situation, as there is always an opportunity for understanding, growth, and discovery of love.

That which appears as a problem is indeed part of the purpose, and part of the solution.

You are not doing anything wrong. You are not blocked. You are exactly where you are meant to be.

Angels, please help me see that all obstacles, challenges, and triggers are the exact pathway that I need to walk now.

Guiding Angels:
Archangel Faith, Archangel Zadkiel, Archangel Haniel

DAY 339

Channelled Angel message

Control, attachment, and worry delay the creation process. Faith, trust and allowing speed it up.

Control contracts your energy. It is fear based, and closes you off to possibility, to guidance and to the miraculous energy of the divine.

Faith is expansive. Faith is rooted in love. It opens your aura to the infinite possibilities of the universal consciousness, of miracles, and of source/God.

Faith allows for infinite possibilities to flow to you at the exact divine perfect moment.

Faith and love are acts of rebellion in a world that is currently operating from a fear-based projection and perspective.

However, as you shift further into the new higher 5D frequencies, accessing this infinite energy current will become easier and easier.

This will become palpably softer and easier after the coming inversion shift.

For now, when you find it hard to let go, we remind you to go to nature.

Angels, when it feels really difficult for me to let go and find faith, please remind me to go to nature so I can feel your loving presence.

Guiding Angels: Archangel Faith

DAY 340

Channelled Angel message

The shift occurring now will result in two realities occurring at once.

This is a shift from 3D to 5D.

The shift is from an inverted, fear- and control-based operating reality, to a heart sovereign, unity-consciousness operating reality.

This shift will result in the veil disintegrating.

The shift will have an overlap period where it seems as if there are two distinct and very different realities occurring at once.

This will feel confusing and surreal at times, but it is all as it should be.

Each human plays a divinely perfect part now, as always.

There is no right or wrong. There is only a different perspective.

Connection and unity are always available.

Remember that love, acceptance, compassion, and unity are the path now.

Invocation

Angels, as I navigate this changing reality, please help me embody all that I wish to see in the world. Please help me embody grace.

Guiding Angels: Archangel Grace

DAY 341

Channelled Angel message

Everything is created from the energy of love. And so, love is the only answer.

The energy of creation—the current that runs through all living beings, through all nature and the infinite universal consciousness—is love.

Love is that which creates.

All that you desire is possible with love.

Your capacity to love is limitless, and virtually untapped.

Your ability to work with the energy of love is powerful, for you are made of and one with this energy.

You are both the creator and the miracle.

You are powerful, in the sense that power is the energy of love that radiates through you and from you.

And so, with each question, the answer will always be found in love.

———— Invocation ————

Angels, please remind me that my power is love,
and so I am safe to be powerful.

Guiding Angels:
Archangel Jophiel, Archangel Chamuel, Archangel Michael

DAY 342

Channelled Angel message

Faith and love are the same. You cannot have one without the other.

You are love. Everything about you was created with, is fuelled by and is an expression of love.

Resistance to faith creates resistance to love.

Faith is unity consciousness.

Faith is allowing the energy of love/light to be fully expressed from you, and through you.

Faith is not religious and has no rules or boundaries.

Faith is love expressed infinitely and received infinitely.

The shift you are experiencing now is one of faith.

To experience faith, allow yourself to give and receive love.

——————— Invocation ———————

Angels, please help me let go and have faith. Please help me see that love is the pathway to faith.

Guiding Angels: Archangel Faith, Archangel Chamuel

DAY 343

Channelled Angel message

You are supported by infinite love/light energy above and below.

You are meant to be in constant energetic flow and circuitry with the earth, and the divine.

Your energy body receives love/light energy from Mother Gaia below you, and from source/God above you.

This love/light energy is the same energy that creates stars and created you.

It is pure love.

The shift you are experiencing now is one of consciously reconnecting your energy system and reactivating a permanent connection to the earth, and to the divine.

This is your natural state.

No longer will you need to 'ground' to the earth.

No longer will you need to intentionally 'connect' with the divine.

This shift is occurring now for all living beings.

You are safe to experience this flow of love through your heart now.

You are safe to recall and embody your fully expressed magnificence now.

Things will feel easier as you allow this constant flow to operate in circuitry through you. For this source of energy is and was always available to you and is now able to be received by all.

———————— Invocation ————————

Angels, please help me integrate and open to a full-circuit chakra/ energy-centre connection with both the earth and the divine now.

Guiding Angels: Archangel Metatron, Archangel Gersisa

DAY 344

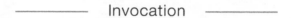

Channelled Angel message

There is an infinite energy supply available to you. It is love.

Love is the energy of creation, of miracles, of inspiration, of music, of laughter, of sadness, of life.

Love is the energy at the centre of all things, and all beings.

Love is energy. A current that can create life from nothing.

Love, when fully understood and expressed, is that which creates the universe and can heal all.

Every answer you seek can be found in exploration of love and resistance to love.

Self-love will bring you power (as love) and full soul expression.

Fully expressed love for others will transform your

relationships.

Love as your guide will show you the steps to your healing pathway.

In every situation, love is the answer and also the energetic current connecting you to all you interact with.

You are a being that is the physical expression of love. You are powerful (filled with the power of love).

Your heart is your guide now. Open your heart to receive and experience the power of love.

─────── Invocation ───────

Angels, please help me let go of all fears around giving and receiving love.

Guiding Angels: Archangel Michael, Archangel Chamuel

DAY 345

Channelled Angel message

Love is flooding Earth like never before. It will reveal all that is hidden.

Prepare for revelations and clarity as all veils are removed now.

All is not as it seems, and all will be revealed in divine perfect timing by the light of source.

The frequency of Earth is rising in a rapid acceleration now.

Love/light is exponentially anchoring through the hearts of all beings.

The collective consciousness is shifting. The veil is dismantling.

Soon all will become visible. Within and without.

For some, this will come as a shock. For others, it will be a relief.

All is as it should be.

All is well.

Allow the love/light to be received and anchored in your own sovereign heart now.

─────── Invocation ───────

Angels, please help me be present to the shift occurring now as it is asking to be expressed in my own being.

Guiding Angels:
Archangel Chamuel, Archangel Metatron, Archangel Butyalil

DAY 346

Channelled Angel message

Breaking free from fear is possible by reconnecting with the infinite source of love.

Death is not the ending. You are eternal. Once you recall this fact in its full truth, you will no longer fear death.

Death is a reunion with the universal one consciousness, from which you are not separate.

This life is not the only expression of consciousness you have had, nor will you have.

Fear closes your heart. Your heart is your connection with the one thing that reminds you of your full magnificent power. Love.

Love is available to you as both a feeling and an energy source. It is a language and a frequency. It heals you and comforts you. It is your energy current, it creates life, and it is the magic ingredient in all that you imagine/create into existence.

And so, the most important thing you can do is explore love.

Fear will become a distant memory as you open your heart and reconnect with the universal source of all love.

You are safe to open your heart and reconnect with the divine now.

*Angels, please help me let go of all fear of fully feeling and
expressing the love that is within me.*

Guiding Angels: Archangel Michael, Archangel Chamuel

DAY 347

Channelled Angel message

Your heart is the key to your connection with the divine, and all living beings. You connect via love.

Love is the energy of all creation.

All life is an expression of love in form.

You are an expression of love in form.

You are not separate from any other. All are one consciousness.

You are not separate from the divine. You are an expression of the divine in form.

You can communicate with the divine, with us, and with all conscious beings.

The medium for your communication is love.

You are powerful beyond measure. Power is love expressed as energy, as current.

As you open your heart now, you experience a reconnection with the universal consciousness.

You are safe to open your heart to the infinite love that flows through all.

You are safe to connect with the divine.

Love is your birthright, intuition is your birthright, full soul expression is your birthright.

Fear is receding now.

Love is anchoring now.

Angels, please help me adjust to the increasing experiences of blissful and infinite love.

Guiding Angels:
Archangel Michael, Archangel Uriel, Archangel Chamuel

DAY 348

Channelled Angel message

We will never make you feel shame or fear. Our messages are always empowering, accepting, and loving.

As you begin to open your heart to the divine, and work with us, you will find resistance and old programming.

You will at times encounter fear of using your intuition.

You may find old programming or stories that it is unsafe or wrong to work with us.

You may be afraid of opening up and receiving unwanted messages from other sources.

Working with your intuition with our guidance is safe. It is also always a positive experience.

We are bound to respect your free will.

We love you unconditionally. We accept you exactly as you are, and love and accept you more than you can fully comprehend.

We will never predict your future. This would violate your free will.

We will never be upset with you, angry with you, or disappointed. Ever.

We will never make you feel ashamed of your actions. We will always remind you that every single experience has a reason and purpose.

We will mirror your highest pathway and your power back to

you always.

We will show you your capacity and your ability to love, always.

We will remind you of your strength, always.

We love you.

———— Invocation ————

Angels, please help me unlock and release any final veils, stories or beliefs that are preventing me from receiving your loving guidance now.

Guiding Angels:
Archangel Michael, Archangel Uriel, Archangel Raziel

DAY 349

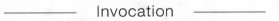

You are experiencing a full mind/body/spirit frequency shift.

This shift is already underway.

It is taking you from a 3D experience to a 5D experience.

This will both require and create change from every aspect of your mind/body/spirit reality.

This shift will occur within, and without.

Your consciousness is evolving. Your perception, ideas, identity, and ability to learn and create are all changing now. The shift is from an external authority to internal heart sovereignty.

Your connection to the divine is evolving. You are now in energetic circuitry above and below. This will open your extrasensory perception and your intuition and bring you into unity-consciousness awareness.

Your physical experience and how you understand everything from a physical level is evolving. Healing, wellness, energy, strength, and loving physical intimacy will all change.

The shift, in all aspects, will be and is quantum.

Allow yourself space and time to experience this miraculous shift now.

———————— Invocation ————————

Angels, please remind me that this shift is exactly what I chose to experience, and that all is well.

Guiding Angels:
Archangel Faith, Archangel Metatron

DAY 350

Angel lesson: Archangel Grace

Archangel Grace has a calming energy that envelopes you with compassion, acceptance, and a gentle love that neutralise all fear, all resistance, all walls, and all control.

Working with Archangel Grace invites you to practice surrender, knowing that in your leap of faith, you will find the divine.

You will find grace.

When you connect with Archangel Grace you will feel all your self-judgement dissolve, replaced by compassion, forgiveness, unconditional love, and acceptance.

When you connect with Archangel Grace you will feel all your final veils, attachments, and outdated belief systems dissolve instantly.

When you connect with Archangel Grace you will feel a sense of peace in the discomfort of change. You will feel your loving power, your divinity, your worth, and the infinite love of the divine holding you.

Peace is found, self-acceptance and acceptance for others blossoms in your heart and consciousness.

Archangel Grace invites you to open to the miracle of connecting to all beings with an open and loving heart, knowing that what is for you comes to you in divine perfect timing, and to lovingly accept and let go of all that is not here right now, for this is also in divine perfect order.

Archangel Grace assists you to find inner strength and courage, to gently openly your heart to deeper loving connections with all beings, whilst feeling safe and held by the love of the divine.

—————— Invocation ——————

Archangel Grace, I invite you to work with me now. Please help me find acceptance for all that exists in my life right now in this moment. Please help me see the divine perfection and love in all my experiences and embody grace.

Guiding Angel: Archangel Grace
Energy: Feminine
Aura colour: Soft yellow and pink

DAY 351

Channelled Angel message

The shift is continuous. Each moment is a shift.

You are experiencing a shift in consciousness that is of a quantum nature.

This shift requires reprogramming from a 3D operating reality to a 5D operating reality (or frequency).

Making this shift is not a singular event or moment. There is no one day or event when everything will be different.

The shift is incremental and exponential, as a frequency expands.

The shift is experienced in your perception, your awareness, your energy, and your physical body.

The shift is practised, felt, and noticed.

The shift will only be apparent after the fact, for it requires realisation.

You can experience ease during this shift by bringing your attention and awareness to each moment, noticing the old programming, and choosing to curiously look at things from a different perspective.

Love is the shift. Love is the pathway. Love is the circuit breaker which will assist you to reprogram now.

--------- Invocation ---------

Angels, please help me let go of attachment to and expectation of external change and be present to the experience I am having now in this moment.

Guiding Angels:
Guardian Angels, Archangel Faith, Archangel Metatron

DAY 352

Channelled Angel message

This shift is from separation to unity. The shift is mind/body/spirit.

The shift you are experiencing is so significant that it will feel like an altered state of consciousness.

Every human has only known one way of experiencing reality: separation.

Now, with the current frequency shift, unity is being

remembered.

Every human remembers unity, as unity is love, and all life is created from the energy of love.

As the shift occurs, everything that has been created from a place of separation will be thrown into the spotlight for rebirthing from a place of unity.

This process has begun and is accelerating.

The new frequency cannot and will not sustain separation-based constructs.

Your own perception will also shift from separation to unity, and all beliefs and stories that were formed from a perspective of separation will require reinventing.

We can assist you with this shift.

─────── Invocation ───────

Angels, please help me open my heart and mind to receive and realise my higher memory of unity now.

Guiding Angels: Archangel Butyalil, Archangel Chamuel

DAY 353

Channelled Angel message

You are remembering your infinite limitlessness now.

There are no boundaries or limits to your experience here, now.

Your perception and awareness are shifting and enabling you to realise this now.

Each wave and shift brings new awareness to your true self.

This is as much an unlearning as it is a remembering.

This is an awakening.

You remember this state of unity in your heart.

You are safe to let go of the many blocks, programs, patterns, walls, and beliefs that have kept you safe, yet disconnected.

Your full power is safe to feel and express. This power is love.

This process is occurring for all beings in waves, at a speed and pace perfect for each individual.

This process is a mind, body, and spirit shift.

You are re-calibrating to a new frequency that is love.

This requires unlocking from an old frequency that is fear.

———— Invocation ————

Angels, please help me gently navigate my own journey of removing all veils and opening to be an expression of infinite love now.

Guiding Angels:
Archangel Haniel, Archangel Metatron, Archangel Michael

DAY 354

Channelled Angel message

Everything that you have been told is impossible is possible.

The current reality is created from an inverted perspective based on fear, control, external authority, disconnection, and separation.

This reality is limited in its ability to create as it is not connected with the divine flow of universal love.

This reality uses fear as a method of control and to hypnotise and distract you from the truth.

The truth is that all beings are divine co-creators. All beings are able to create and manifest instantly when connected with universal source energy. All beings are one consciousness. All beings are love/light expressed in form. All beings are able to experience bliss, genius, magic, unity, peace, unconditional love, healing and realisation.

And so, as you become aware of this inversion, we invite you to also experience a shift within your own consciousness.

As you awaken, you remember that you are sovereign and no other can create your reality.

As you awaken, you remember love is your birthright.

As you awaken, you remember that you are powerful beyond your imagining.

As you awaken, you experience a reconnection with the divine unity of the one consciousness.

As you awaken, you remember that the impossible is indeed possible.

———— Invocation ————

Angels, please help me identify and let go of all remaining limiting beliefs, so that I can fully embrace my radiant potential now.

Guiding Angels:
Archangel Michael, Archangel Haniel, Archangel Metatron

DAY 355

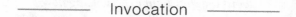
Channelled Angel message

Now and in every moment forwards, separation is dissolving.

The shift you are experiencing is a reconnection to the divine one consciousness.

In every moment from now onwards, you will find it easier to give and receive love.

In every moment from now onwards, you will feel more connected to all living beings.

In every moment from now onwards, you will notice the veil

is thinning.

In every moment from now onwards, you will become aware that the other is you, and all are one.

In every moment from now onwards, you will see that fear no longer has power.

In every moment from now onwards, you will trust your heart and your own wisdom above all others.

In every moment from now onwards, you will be shifting awareness from fear to love, from resistance to faith, from external authority to sovereign heart freedom.

———— Invocation ————

Angels, please help me let go of all my remaining fears about the shift I am experiencing now.

Guiding Angels: Archangel Michael

DAY 356

Channelled Angel message

The shift you are experiencing will make it easier for you to see and feel new pathways.

As the frequency shifts now, fear dissipates and love anchors.

As the frequency shifts now, the fear programming begins to glitch, and falter.

You will find it easier to see clearly in your perception of the world around you, and also in your personal awareness and thought programming.

Old fear-based programs and stories will no longer hold as true.

You will be able to notice these old thought patterns more easily and choose not to allow them to anchor as reality.

You will be able to see deception and lies in the world around you more easily.

Most importantly, you will find it easier to choose a new pathway in any given moment, and make choices based on love, acceptance, and unity.

This process is anchoring now and will become easier and easier as the 5D love/light frequency shift accelerates.

Pay attention and stay present now. All will slowly become crystal clear.

─────── Invocation ───────

Angels, please help me trust the process and let go of all remaining resistance and control now.

Guiding Angels: Archangel Michael, Archangel Faith

DAY 357

Channelled Angel message

New Earth is birthed by repeated acts of choosing love over fear.

The shift is not a one-time event. It is a continuous reprogramming, a reconnection, a remembering.

The shift expands in waves as the collective consciousness awakens.

The shift is experienced in moments. Each moment an individual chooses to react from love rather than fear, the light anchors and grows.

New Earth requires a rebellion of love.

New Earth requires your love. Your rebellion.

Rebellion against fear, and continuous rebellious acts of love.

Love is always the answer, in every moment. Especially when it seems the most difficult or impossible thing to do.

The frequency has softened now, and the infinite love of the divine is more easily accessible than ever before.

Our love and guidance are accessible more than ever before.

Love is more accessible than ever before.

Invocation

Angels, please help me release all my remaining fear programs so that I can experience infinite love now.

Guiding Angels: Archangel Michael, Archangel Chamuel

DAY 358

Channelled Angel message

As the veil thins now, you will become aware of all that was created from fear. And you will awaken to the infinite love of the divine.

The inversion and shift in consciousness occurring now requires becoming aware of all that was created from the 3D perspective of fear.

In balance to this process is the heart awakening and reconnection to the infinite divine love.

Separation is disintegrating now. Unity is birthing now.

This process will take time. It will feel at times as if everything that exists is now distorted or inverted. And then, at times it will feel as if love has never felt more powerful, connection has never been easier, empathy has never felt so intense, and the divine has never felt so present.

This process will occur in waves, and will require adjustment, shifts and integration along the way.

Shadows come to light to be transformed and reborn. This is the pathway to New Earth.

Healing, compassion, acceptance, and love are the pathway to New Earth.

You are not alone. You never were. Now you will remember and feel this love!

--------- Invocation ---------

Angels, please help me integrate and acclimatise to the shifts and changes that are occurring now in my mind, body, and spirit.

Guiding Angels: Archangel Metatron

DAY 359

Channelled Angel message

All deception, shadows and veils will be illuminated now.

The illusion of fear and separation is crumbling and dismantling.

As part of this process, all that has been created from this inverted perspective will come into clarity and focus.

This will occur within and without, for both the individual and the collective consciousness.

Clarity will come instantly. Suddenly, all will become clear.

This will occur in waves. And be repeated until all has come to light.

Shock, pain, and grief may occur as part of this revelation process. This is necessary.

Go gently. Love heals all now.

Compassion, acceptance, and forgiveness are the pathway now.

Unconditional love and unity are the pathway now.

Angels, please help me through my own process of clearly seeing all that has been hidden and veiled both within my own heart and my perception of the world around me. Please help me find compassion, forgiveness, and acceptance for all the darkness that I see.

Guiding Angels:
Archangel Zadkiel, Archangel Haniel, Archangel Michael

DAY 360

Channelled Angel message

We invite you to repair and heal your soul connection with the divine.

The frequency on Earth has shifted to a higher love/light percentage now.

This frequency shift brings Earth and all living beings into a new frequency, one never experienced before.

This new energy is creating mind/body/spirit changes.

These changes are anchored in love/light and will shift the collective consciousness gradually from duality to unity.

This process will occur at the divine right time for each individual, and is gradual, occurring in waves.

This process will result in each individual soul experiencing healing, and the collective also experiencing healing.

The healing time has begun. This process is one of accepting shadows and light, and compassionate acceptance of the full spectrum of the current collective expression of consciousness.

No shadow can be ignored now, for the individual or the collective. No shadow can be hidden now.

Healing can be instant now. All it takes is realisation, and loving acceptance.

Ask for a sacred guide or healer to assist you if needed.

Your connection to the divine is easier to feel than ever before.

In time, all will awaken and reconnect to the source of infinite love/light, and a new expression of consciousness will birth along the way.

This is the journey to New Earth.

────────── Invocation ──────────

Angels, please help me through my own healing
and awakening now.

Guiding Angels:
Archangel Haniel, Archangel Raphael, Archangel Uriel

DAY 361

Channelled Angel message

The shift occurring now is an awakening. A remembering of unity consciousness and infinite love.

As the frequency shifts now, there is a spontaneous shift in consciousness occurring.

This shift is an awakening.

All will awaken at their divine perfect moment.

All are at different stages, and acceptance of these different paces is needed for unity consciousness to anchor now.

The awakening is a reconnection of the sacred heart to the infinite one consciousness. It is an inversion of the perception of separation, and a realisation of unity.

The shift is accelerated by expressions of love, by healing, by forgiveness and acceptance.

The shift is accelerated by unconditional love for self and

others.

The shift is accelerated by sovereign and rebellious self-expression and acts of love.

All you need to do now is be you, and be loving. It's all you ever needed to do.

———————— Invocation ————————

Angels, please remind me that the process of my shift is in fact very simple. Please remind me to be love.

Guiding Angels:
Archangel Butyalil, Archangel Chamuel, Archangel Metatron

DAY 362

Channelled Angel message

Your choices and actions now create New Earth.

You are the creator.

Your dreams, desires, hopes and actions are powerful beyond your wildest imagining.

Even though it may seem at times as if you are all alone, and could not possibly make an impact, we want you to know that this couldn't be further from the truth.

Your vision is true.

Your sense of a new earth birthing is true.

You have the sight for a reason; now it is time to honour your vision and take action.

Your actions need not seem monumental. Every action that honours your own pathway to light is powerful.

Integrity and sovereignty are your guiding light now.

Hope and faith are your pathway now.

It has never been more important to be you, express you, and be true to your own heart guidance now.

Small steps matter now. And you will not take them alone. We are with you, always. Even and especially when you can't feel us.

New Earth is birthed by you, through you now.

Every day, in every moment and every step, become and embody the world that you wish to see, and reject that which you know is dying now.

Turn your back on the inverted fear-based world now and turn towards the light.

You do not walk alone.

--------- Invocation ---------

Angels, please stand with me, protect me, uplift me, and guide me as I walk the path to embodiment of unity now.

Guiding Angels: Archangel Butyalil, Archangel Michael

DAY 363
Channelled Angel message

Faith and surrender operate on divine timing. You cannot control the divine.

All that you desire now lies on the other side of surrender.

Letting go and trusting the divine now is the most important action you can take.

Faith requires walking towards that which has no guarantee of success, feels risky and uncertain, and requires a belief in something bigger than yourself.

Faith is an act of love, and of surrender.

You cannot force surrender, or faith.

Every soul has their own divine moment of surrender that is life changing and opens their heart to the divine deeper than they imagined possible.

This is the time to be opening to surrender and deepening your faith now.

It is your highest priority.

You are safe to let go, and welcome in the divine now.

You are safe to trust.

You are safe to have faith.

——————— Invocation ———————

Angels, please help me walk through the walls of my own fears and resistance, so that I can find surrender, faith, and the infinite support of the divine.

Guiding Angels:
Archangel Faith, Archangel Michael, Archangel Uriel

DAY 364

Channelled Angel message

New Earth births in ongoing waves of healing, expansion, and integration.

The shift you are experiencing is not a one-time event.

The shift you are experiencing is not complete.

In fact, it has barely begun.

The shift is growing exponentially now, and each wave will create change that you cannot even conceive of yet.

Change will occur in your mind, body, and spirit experience, as well as all around you in the collective.

Your focus now is the light.

Hold your vision, even as everything seems to continue to intensify, crumble and fall around you.

Great change cannot occur without great change.

Change is rarely easy.

Rebirth occurs as part of the cycle of life, and this also includes decay and death.

Do not be afraid of the coming changes, for they are needed, for all.

Hold steady to your powerful heart truth now. Your vision is true.

———————— Invocation ————————

Angels, please help me find peace and acceptance with the death of the old that I witness within my own experience and my external reality now.

Guiding Angels:
Archangel Azrael, Archangel Nathaniel, Archangel Chamuel

DAY 365

Channelled Angel message

There is always light. To find the light, look for that which you love.

Even when there is great change around you, the light is present.

Even when there are great challenges, the light is present.

Even when there is death, the light is present.

The light is in the sun, the birds, the ocean, and the wind.

The light is in your loved ones, your family, and your friends.

The light is in you.

Love/light exists in every moment. Even when it seems absent.

Love/light is a flame that cannot be extinguished. It burns always within your own heart.

Love/light is an energy, a current, that exists within every living being, every plant, and every natural occurrence in your world.

Love/light is a frequency that is available for you to connect to and access, as a reminder of unity, of your magnificence, of your origins and of your potential. You can access this in any divine moment, simply by remembering that it is within you.

You can shift from fear to love in any given moment by realising that you are love.

Divine being, we love you, we are an aspect of you, and you are an aspect of us.

We are one.

————— Invocation —————

Angels, thank you for loving me unconditionally so that I can learn to love myself unconditionally.

Guiding Angels: All Angels

Reference

The New Angels

Archangels:

There are potentially an unlimited number of Archangels, however there are 35 Archangels who more commonly work with us. Archangels work with us on an individual *and* collective level and have specific themes or focus areas. Of these, 15 Archangels asked to share their new messages with the world and are included in individual lessons in the pages of this book (page numbers for each Archangel lesson are below).

1. Amethyst
2. Ariel pg. 147
3. Azrael pg. 75
4. Aurora
5. Butyalil pg. 189
6. Chamuel pg. 68
7. Christiel
8. Christine
9. Faith pg. 110
10. Fhelyai
11. Gabriel
12. Gaia
13. Gersisa pg. 56
14. Grace pg. 402
15. Haniel pg. 154
16. Jeremiel
17. Jophiel pg. 95
18. Joules
19. Lailah
20. Mallory
21. Mariel
22. Mary
23. Metatron pg. 198
24. Michael pg. 49
25. Moroni
26. Nathaniel pg. 39
27. Purlimiek
28. Raguel
29. Raphael pg. 27
30. Raziel
31. Roquiel
32. Sandalphon pg. 124
33. Uriel pg. 106
34. Voku Monak
35. Zadkiel

Collective Angels:

Collective Angels are groups of Angels who work together to assist humanity in specific focus areas. Some rarely interact with humans on an individual level (Seraphim, Cherubim, Thrones, Dominions, Powers, Principalities). Some are very active now as we move through the current ascension portal (Record Keeper Angels).

1. Seraphim Angels
2. Cherubim Angels
3. Throne Angels
4. Dominion Angels
5. Power Angels
6. Principality Angels
7. Virtue Angels
8. Messenger Angels
9. Record Keeper Angels

Guardian Angels:

Guardian Angels are different from both Archangels and the Collective Angels, and work with us on an individual level only. Every human has 2-4 Guardian Angels who have been assisting them through every earthly incarnation.

You can find three specific Guardian Angel lessons on pages 20, 30 & 72 of this book.

You can also find lessons on Angel communication and signs on pages 31 & 71.

Glossary of terms

3D/3rd density: The 3rd frequency level of human consciousness where separation, lack, limits, linear time, and the physical aspects of the human experience are explored in order to expand and raise consciousness and ascend into a higher state of awareness and expression. When a being becomes self-aware in 3rd density, they then begin the journey through 4th and into 5th density. 3D is a harder/more intense earthly experience which can rapidly catalyse spiritual growth and awareness. 3rd density consciousness is unable to see through the veil and is rarely aware of other dimensions/realities/beings. We are at the end of a 75,000-year cycle exploring 3rd density.

4D/4th density: 4D consciousness is reached when a being chooses service to others over service to self and discovers and embodies their purpose. In 4th density human consciousness expands to enable an exploration of the non-physical, and the ability to see beyond the veil. The journey to sovereignty and individualization begins in 4D consciousness.

5D/5th density: 5D consciousness is embodiment of unity consciousness, acceptance, compassion, forgiveness, and unconditional love. 5D is consciousness is connected to the infinite and all beings and allows one to be a conduit or channel for creation, evolution, and change. 5D requires balanced polarity between masculine and feminine energies, and an acceptance of the necessary balance of shadow and light.5D is birthing now.

9D/9th & 10D/10th density: The Angels haven't shared much with me about 9th and 10th density yet, other than that the Guardian Angels exist at 9th density, and the Archangels exist at 10th density. The Angels have told me that these frequencies are beyond our comprehension at this stage of our awareness, and that the Angels exist from 9th density and above.

Ascension: the process of intentionally raising your vibration and expanding your consciousness via the human experience. Ascension is realised over many lifetimes, with the ultimate goal of ascending, or no longer incarnating in physical form.

Awakening: The process of becoming self-aware, or spiritually aware, often occurring as a being shifts from 3D to 4D awareness and frequency.

Clairsentience: Clear feeling

Claircognicence: Clear knowing

Clairaudience: Clear hearing

Clairvoyance: Clear seeing

Chakras: the energy centres that exist in the physical and light body.

DNA/Light body activation: a shift that occurs on a cellular level as a result of an energetic frequency upgrade, which then upgrades our dormant DNA, and triggers a gradual physical, energetic and consciousness shift to crystalline or 5D human expression.

Elementals: Benevolent beings who maintain harmony and balance with nature, such as gnomes, goblins, pixies, brownies, and sylphs. Presided over by Archangel Ariel.

Energetic vampirism/energy vampires: Intentional or unintentional harvesting of life force energy from another being. Beings who harvest life force energy from another being.

False light Matrix/light matrix: a set of systems, structures, organisations, and beliefs intentionally inserted into our collective consciousness and society with the intention of inverting and controlling the true human potential, and inner light.

Heart guidance: intuitive knowing that is felt and understood via energetic communication within the heart, activated by a sense of deep love, and feelings of joy.

Light body: Your energetic, or holographic body which records all your earthly experiences in the Akashic record. The light body is overlayed over/within the physical body and exists eternally. Within the light body are your chakras, your soul spark, and your full higher consciousness. The light body is surrounded by a large auric field of energy which interacts with all beings on a frequency level. All communication with the non-physical is done via the light body as a form of energetic transmission.

Light codes: information from source encoded in light to activate shifts in frequency and awareness.

Light worker: Any being who has a soul mission to bring light to the world through service to others.

Mission activation: an experience that triggers a soul or higher-self memory of your purpose or mission, chosen before incarnation.

New earth: A term used in the spiritual community to symbolise the rebirth of human consciousness and actualisation of a new earth reality based on unity, and unconditional love. New earth is not a physical location, but a state of consciousness birthing now through you.

Quantum field: On a spiritual level this refers to a zero-point state outside of linear time and space where all possibilities, dimensions, times, and realities exist simultaneously.

Quantum healing: Healing that occurs on all levels, times, realities, and dimensions.

Quantum time: A spiritual concept of non-linear time where all times, dimensions and realities exist at once.

Shadow healing/shadow work: the process of uncovering, expressing, and healing your hidden emotions, beliefs, identities, and wounds, which can lead to deeper understanding of self, more authentic expression, and awakening.

Soul contract: an agreement made prior to incarnation to have a significant life experience with another person.

Soul family: describes the instant knowing or connection one feels when they recognise a person as having originated from the same soul group or pod prior to incarnation.

Starseed: A being who originated from a different star system prior to incarnation on earth. The mission of the starseed is to awaken to and express their unique gifts and vision to the world, experienced in a different reality.

Timeline: A potential future or past manifestation of reality. All timelines exist at once in the quantum field, and all manifestation occurs via timelines. When we receive a future vision, we are drawing down information from a potential or future timeline and have free will to then manifest this into reality.

Timeline balancing: healing past, future, and potential experiences which can cause ripples and shifts in time.

The great awakening: a term used to denote a time of the predicted mass spiritual awakening of humanity.

Unity consciousness: an experience of consciousness where separation and other are realised as false, and one-ness and unity are actualised in the collective consciousness. Unity consciousness is realised via the awakening and ascension process and is an expression of 5D or unconditional love.

About the author

Shunanda Scott

Angel medium, ascension guide and mother of three Shunanda Scott is passionate about teaching people how to receive the infinitely loving guidance and support of the Angels.

Upon the birth of her second child, Shunanda experienced a spiritual awakening and began learning how to manage her newly discovered intuitive abilities. Shunanda trained for years with mentors, teachers, and the Angels themselves, and now works with starseeds and lightworkers all over the world from her beach home in Sydney.

The New Angel Messages is a collection of sacred daily Angel transmissions received by Shunanda—each message sent with love to guide humanity through the current collective journey of transformation and awakening.

CPSIA information can be obtained
at www.ICGtesting.com
Printed in the USA
BVHW030959160222
629066BV00019B/24